14 Days

BY ROBERT EMMET SHERWOOD

THERE SHALL BE NO NIGHT

ABE LINCOLN IN ILLINOIS

IDIOT'S DELIGHT

THE PETRIFIED FOREST

REUNION IN VIENNA

THIS IS NEW YORK

THE VIRTUOUS KNIGHT

WATERLOO BRIDGE

THE QUEEN'S HUSBAND

THE ROAD TO ROME

CHARLES SCRIBNER'S SONS

There Shall Be No Night

by

ROBERT E. SHERWOOD

Few plays written in our time have made such a stirring impact upon the minds and emotions of audiences as "There Shall Be No Night." In this story of Dr. Kaarlo Valkonen, an eminent Finnish scientist, his wife and son, and what befell them in a desperately embattled country, Robert Sherwood has written a play of supreme timeliness, at once deeply significant and breathlessly exciting. Here is the complete play that was greeted with unrestrained enthusiasm by playgoers and critics—a drama that comes through the printed page in all its compelling power.

"Enormously impressive. It speaks for the truth with enkindling faith and passionate conviction." *Brooks Atkinson* in *The New York Times*

"A moving play . . . written beautifully and with intensity . . . enriched by feeling and sympathy." *Richard Lockridge* in *The New York Sun*

"An absorbing play . . . vivid and stirring . . . what he shows us is an incredible example of gallantry in the face of overwhelming odds. . . . It moves with emotional conviction."

John Anderson in *The New York Journal-American*

"It is a drama of our time . . . as thrillingly dramatic as any story your commentator may tell you over the radio or your paper's editor print on his first page." *Burns Mantle* in *The New York Daily News*

"It is a play of stature, dignity and high emotion, thoughtful, eloquent and heartfelt. It has something of great contemporary import to say to what we call our civilization, and it speaks from both the mind and heart." *Richard Watts, Jr.,* in *The New York Herald Tribune*

THERE SHALL BE NO NIGHT

BY

ROBERT E. SHERWOOD

NEW YORK

CHARLES SCRIBNER'S SONS

1941

THIS PLAY IS DEDICATED

WITH MY LOVE

TO MY WIFE

MADELINE

"There Shall Be No Night" was produced and presented by The Playwrights' Company—Maxwell Anderson, S. N. Behrman, Elmer Rice, Robert E. Sherwood—and The Theatre Guild—for the first time at the Opera House in Providence, R. I., on March 29th, 1940, with the following cast:

DR. KAARLO VALKONEN	Alfred Lunt
MIRANDA VALKONEN	Lynn Fontanne
DAVE CORWEEN	Richard Whorf
UNCLE WALDEMAR	Sydney Greenstreet
GUS SHUMAN	Brooks West
ERIK VALKONEN	Montgomery Clift
KAATRI ALQUIST	Elisabeth Fraser
DR. ZIEMSSEN	Maurice Colbourne
MAJOR RUTKOWSKI	Edward Raquello
JOE BURNETT	Charles Ansley
BEN GICHNER	Thomas Gomez
FRANK OLMSTEAD	William Le Massena
SERGEANT GOSDEN	Claude Horton
LEMPI	Phyllis Thaxter
ILMA	Charva Chester
PHOTOGRAPHER	Ralph Nelson
PHOTOGRAPHER	Robert Downing

Staged by Alfred Lunt.

Settings designed by Richard Whorf.

vii

THERE SHALL BE NO NIGHT

SCENES

I. Living room of the Valkonens' house in Helsinki. Early in October, 1938.

(Intermission)

II. The same. Late in November, 1939.

III. The same. The next day.

IV. The same. January 1, 1940.

(Intermission)

V. Dave Corween's rooms in the Hotel Kamp, in Helsinki. Late in February.

VI. Classroom in a schoolhouse near the west shore of Viipuri Bay. A few days later.

VII. The Valkonens' living room. A few days later.

PREFACE

After the first performance of "There Shall Be No Night" in Providence, Rhode Island, on March 29, 1940, a young man, a stranger, came up to me and said, "You certainly have changed your point of view since 'Idiot's Delight.'" There was a distinct note of accusation in his voice. This was the first of many similar and many less temperate accusations which this play has provoked. Having identified myself time and again in the past as a pacifist, I had now become a "Warmonger."

It is a strange fact that many people who can bear with equanimity all sorts of assaults upon their moral character or their personal habits are goaded to indignant counter-attack when they are charged with inconsistency. "I don't mind being called a black-hearted villain, an enemy of society. In fact, I might even be flattered by such distinction. But—by God—I'll fight any man who dares to imply that I have been untrue to myself."

Therefore, I wish to preface this play with a review of the development of my own point of view, as it has been expressed in other plays. I want to say that "There Shall Be No Night" is not a denial of "Idiot's Delight": it is a sequel. I realize that there is an appreciable difference be-

tween what I have written and what I have tried
to write. But I shall deal in this Preface with my
motives, and the nature of the experience which
impelled them.

As a common soldier in the Canadian army in
the first World War, in training camps, in the
line, in hospitals, and in clinks, I was mixed in
with men from all over the British Empire and the
United States. In one hospital the occupant of the
bed on one side of mine was an Australian who
had been horribly burned by liquid fire in the
crater at Loos three years before. In the bed on
the other side of mine was a South African Jew;
a machine gun bullet had lodged in the base of his
spine and he knew he would never walk again. It
was a great surprise to me to discover that these
two men, and all other men whom I got to know
well, thought and talked and acted and reacted
just about as I did. What was so surprising about
it was the revelation of the narrowness and shal-
lowness of my own mind. I had been brought up
to believe that because I was a 100 per cent American—and a Harvard man, at that—I was superior.

At the age of twenty-two my career as a soldier was ended—for all time, as I then hopefully
believed. I became a veteran, and as such recap-
tured a certain sense of superiority. (That didn't
last long, either. Never was there a baser decep-
tion than the famous recruiting poster which
showed a cute little girl pointing a chubby finger

at her father and asking, "Daddy—what did YOU do in the Great War?" As things have turned out, when the children of my generation point the finger at us the one word that follows it is "Sucker!") I took with me out of the army certain convictions, which have stayed with me and which all the dreadful events of the past twenty years have served only to strengthen.

I became internationally minded—and in the opinion of the apostles of isolationism, the word "internationalist" is synonymous with "warmonger." I believed that war was a hideous injustice and that no man had the right to call himself civilized as long as he admitted that another world war could conceivably be justifiable. I believed that the beginning of the elimination of war was the elimination of nationalism, the chauvinistic concept of patriotism. And I believed that the beginning of the elimination of nationalism was in some form of union of the English-speaking peoples who were already united by the advantages of a common language, common traditions of freedom, common ethics, and a common desire for peace.

I was instinctively enthusiastic about the scheme for a League of Nations. I wanted to believe that there would be some medium for expressing the good will that I shared with the scalded Australian and the paralyzed South African Jew. But, in 1919, I was convinced of the futility of the League by the writings of George Harvey and other Wilson-haters. I became a rabid opponent of the League—which means that whenever I engaged in a discussion of the major political issues in some speak-easy I would say "The League won't work because it's impractical. I agree absolutely with Senator Henry Cabot Lodge that Article XVI stinks!" I had a very hazy idea of what Article XVI actually provided for, but I was young and free again and it was much more fun to be a critic than an adherent.

In 1920, I confess with deep shame, my first vote as an American citizen was cast for Warren G. Harding. Thus, I did my bit in the great betrayal. I voted for the proposition that all the American soldiers who had given their lives in the Great War had died in vain. And what I and all other Americans got from Harding's victory was a decade of hypocrisy, corruption, crime, glorification of greed and depravity, to be followed logically by a decade of ascendant Hitlerism.

In 1926 I wrote my first play. My main reason for doing so was that I was about to be thirty years old, and I had read somewhere—I think it was in F.P.A.'s column—that all young newspapermen promise themselves that they will write that play or that novel before they're thirty and then the next thing they know they're forty and still promising. I didn't have time for a novel. When I wrote "The Road to Rome" I didn't know what sort of playwright I might be, provided I might be a playwright at all. So I tried in it every style of dramaturgy—high comedy, low comedy, melodrama, romance (both sacred and profane), hard-boiled realism, beautiful writing—and, of course, I inserted a "message." That message was that I was opposed to war. But any one who remembers "The Road to Rome" remembers it principally for one line, which came near the end of the play. Hannibal, the Carthaginian conqueror, having spent a night with Amytis, the wife of the Roman dictator, Fabius Maximus, has been persuaded by that pleasant experience to spare Rome from destruction. When Hannibal is about to retreat from the Eternal City, the following dialogue occurs:

HANNIBAL

Fabius, I wish happiness and prosperity to you, your wife, and your sons.

FABIUS

Thank you—but I have no sons.

HANNIBAL

You may have . . .

After "The Road to Rome" I made several unsuccessful attempts to repeat the same formula: "a modern comedy in ancient dress." Chief of these was a play (unproduced) called "Marching

As To War." The scene of this was England in the reign of Richard the Lion-hearted and the hero of it was a conscientious objector who refused to go on the Crusade.

In October, 1929—while Prime Minister Ramsay MacDonald was visiting President Herbert Hoover, offering "Faith, Hope and Parity," and Wall Street was just getting ready to crash—I tried another kind of play, "Waterloo Bridge," which was written from my own observations of blacked out, hungry London in 1917. The most important speech in this was spoken by a Canadian soldier. He has just emerged from hospital —an air-raid is going on—and his girl tells him he must go back to France and fight the war. He says:

"Yes—fight the war. What's the war, anyway? It's that guy up there in his aeroplane. What do I care about him and his bombs? What do I care who he is, or what he does, or what happens to him? That war's over for me. What I've got to fight is the whole dirty world. That's the enemy that's against you and me . . ."

"Waterloo Bridge" was almost good. But it was incoherent. Two years after it, I wrote "Reunion in Vienna." I went into this play with what seemed to me an important if not strikingly original idea —science hoist with its own petard—and came out with a gay, romantic comedy. But in the Preface to that play I came closer than I ever had before to a statement of what I was trying to think and write. I quote at length from this Preface, because it has a considerable bearing on all that I have written since then:

"This play is another demonstration of the escape mechanism in operation.

"There is no form of mechanism more popular or in more general use in this obstreperously technological period—which is a sufficient indication of the spirit of moral defeatism that now prevails. It is a spirit, or want of spirit, that can truthfully be said to be new in the world—for the reason that in no previous historic emergency has the common man enjoyed the dubious advantages of consciousness. However unwillingly, he is now able to realize that his generation has the ill-luck to occupy the limbo-like interlude between one age and another. Looking about him, he sees a shell-torn No Man's Land, filled with barbed-wire entanglements and stench and uncertainty. If it is not actual chaos, it is a convincing counterfeit thereof. Before him is black doubt, punctured by brief flashes of ominous light, whose revelations are not comforting. Behind him is nothing but the ghastly wreckage of burned bridges.

"In his desperation, which he assures himself is essentially comic, he casts about for weapons of defense. The old minds offer him Superstition, but it is a stringless bow, impotent in its obsolescence. The new minds offer him Rationalism, but it is a boomerang. He must devise pitiful defenses of his own, like a soldier who spreads a sheet of wrapping paper over his bivouac to keep out the airplane bombs. In Europe, this manifests itself in the heroic but anachronistic attempt to recreate the illusions of nationalism: people drugging themselves with the comforting hope that tomorrow will be a repetition of yesterday, that the Cæsars and the Tudors will return.

"In America, which has had no Cæsars or Tudors, nor even any Hohenzollerns or Habsburgs, the favorite weapon of defense against unlovely reality is a kind of half-hearted cynicism that is increasingly tremulous, increasingly shrill. . . .

"Democracy—liberty, equality, fraternity, and the pursuit of happiness! Peace and prosperity! Emancipation by enlightenment! All the distillations of man's maturing intelligence have gone sour.

"The worst of it is that man had been so full of hope. He had complete confidence in the age of reason, the age of the neutralization of nature, for it was his own idea. It differed from all previous ages in this great respect: it was not caused by the movements of glaciers, the upheaval or submersion of continents, the imposition of prolonged droughts: it was the product of man's restless thought and tireless industry, planned and developed by him not in collaboration with nature but in implacable opposition to it. The reasonings of such as Roger Bacon, Copernicus, Galileo and Newton started the assault upon ignorance, and it has been carried on by countless thinkers and talkers from Voltaire and Rousseau to Shaw and Wells.

"This is the career of the age of reason:

"The eighteenth century knew the excitements of conception, culminating in the supreme orgasm of the French Revolution.

"The nineteenth century was the period of gestation, marred by occasional symptoms of nausea and hysteria and a few dark forebodings, but generally orderly and complacent.

"For the twentieth century have remained the excruciating labor pains and the discovery that the child is a monster; and as modern man looks upon it, and recalls the assurances of the omniscient obstetricians, he is sore distressed. He wishes that with his eyes he could see not, that with his ears he could not hear. But his senses are remarkably acute. . . .

"Man is, for the moment, scornful of the formulæ of the scientists, for he believes that it was they who got him into this mess. To hell with them, and their infallible laws, their experiments noble in motive and disastrous in result, their antiseptic Utopia, their vitamines and their lethal gases, their cosmic rays and their neuroses, all tidily encased in cellophane. To hell with them, says man, but with no relish, for he has been deprived even of faith in the potency of damnation. . . .

"So man is giving loud expression to his reluctance to confront the seemingly inevitable. He is

desperately cherishing the only remaining mani-
festation of the individualism which first distinguished him in the animal kingdom: it is the an-
archistic impulse, rigorously inhibited but still
alive—the impulse to be drunk and disorderly, to
smash laws and ikons, to draw a mustache and
beard on the Mona Lisa, to be a hurler of bombs
and monkey wrenches—the impulse to be an artist
and a damned fool. It was this impulse which
animated Galileo in the face of Romanism and
Lenin in the face of Tsarism, but the disciples of
both of them are determined to exterminate it and
can undoubtedly do so, with the aid of the disciples of Freud. There is no reason why the successful neutralization of nature cannot be ex-
tended to include human nature.

"Man has been clinging to the hope that has
been his since he was delivered from feudalism—
hope that he may live a life which is, in the words
of Whitman, 'copious, vehement, spiritual, bold.'
He is seeing that hope destroyed by instruments
of his own devising, and the reverberations of his
protest are shaking his earth.

"Perhaps this protest is only the last gasp of
primitivism. Perhaps man feels that the traditions of his race demand of him a show of spirit
before he submerges himself in the mass and that,
when the little show is over, he will be glad enough
to fall meekly into line. . . ."

Such were my unhappy thoughts in the winter
of 1931–32, the winter of deepest depression and

of the Lindbergh kidnapping. It was the year
before Hitler came to power.

During the next two years I wrote five plays.
Four of these went right into the bureau drawer,
never to reappear. The fifth, "Acropolis," was
produced in London and failed financially. It has
never been done in the professional theatre in the
United States. It was by all odds the best play
I had written and the most positive affirmation of
my own faith. It was a reaction, a rebellion
against the despairing spirit of the "Reunion in
Vienna" Preface, a rebellion that I have continued ever since. "Acropolis" was another historical
analogy, but a legitimate one. The scene was
Athens in the final years of the Periclean Age,
when the triumph of Athenian democracy was being challenged by Spartan totalitarianism. It
ended with some lines paraphrasing Pericles' fu-
neral oration:

"I cannot give you any of the old words which
say how fair and noble it is to die in battle. But
I can give you the memory of our Commonwealth,
as we have seen it and fallen in love with it, day
by day. I can tell you, with truth, that the story
of our Commonwealth will never die, but will live
on, far away, woven into the fabric of other men's
lives, in a world that is filled not with terror but
with glory. . . ."

Some of these same words are in "There Shall
Be No Night."

Following "Acropolis," I wrote "The Petrified

Forest." This was my first real attempt to write a play about my own country in my own time, to speak out directly. It contained its own Preface. In the following dialogue is the essence of this play:

SQUIER

I don't know anything. You see—the trouble with me is, I belong to a vanishing race. I'm one of the intellectuals.

GABBY

That means you've got brains. I can see you have.

SQUIER

Yes—brains without purpose. Noise without sound. Shape without substance. Have you ever read *The Hollow Men?*

(*She shakes her head.*)

Don't. It's discouraging, because it's true. It refers to the intellectuals, who thought they'd conquered Nature. They dammed it up, and used its waters to irrigate the wastelands. They built streamlined monstrosities to penetrate its resistance. They wrapped it up in cellophane and sold it in drugstores. They were so certain they had it subdued. And now—do you realize what it is that is causing world chaos?

GABBY

No.

SQUIER

Well, I'm probably the only living person who

can tell you. . . . It's Nature hitting back. Not
with the old weapons—floods, plagues, holocausts.
We can neutralize them. She's fighting back with
strange instruments called neuroses. She's delib-
erately afflicting mankind with the jitters. Nature
is proving that she can't be beaten—not by the
likes of us. She's taking the world away from the
intellectuals and giving it back to the apes . . .

Some of this is also in "There Shall Be No
Night."

"The Petrified Forest" was a negative, incon-
clusive sort of play, but I have a great fondness
for it because it pointed me in a new direction, and
that proved to be the way I really wanted to go.

"Idiot's Delight" was written in 1935. It was
about the outbreak of the second World War. It
was completely American in that it represented a
compound of blank pessimism and desperate optimism, of chaos and jazz. It was also representative of its author. I think I can say that completely typical of me was a speech spoken by
Harry Van, an itinerant, small-time showman. He
is conversing with a German bacteriologist, Doctor Waldersee, who is forced by war to end his
experiments on a cancer cure and devote himself
henceforth to the service of his country in dealing
out death. (The same problem as Doctor Valkonen's in "There Shall Be No Night.") Harry
Van tries to reassure this German victim of Naziism.

"I've remained an optimist," he says, "because I'm essentially a student of human nature. You dissect corpses and rats and similar unpleasant things. Well—it has been my job to dissect suckers! I've probed into the souls of some of the Goddamnedest specimens. And what have I found? Now—don't sneer at me, Doctor—but above everything else I've found Faith! Faith in peace on earth, and good will to men—and faith that 'Muma,' the three-legged girl, really has got three legs. All my life, I've been selling phony goods to people of meagre intelligence and great faith. You'd think that would make me contemptuous of the human race, wouldn't you? But—on the contrary—it has given *me* Faith. It has made me sure that no matter how much the meek may be bulldozed or gypped—they *will* eventually inherit the earth."

"Idiot's Delight" was certainly an anti-war play; it was also violently anti-Fascist. In its postscript I wrote: "If people will continue to be intoxicated by the synthetic spirit of patriotism, pumped into them by megalomaniac leaders, and will continue to have faith in the 'security' provided by those lethal weapons sold to them by the armaments industry, then war is inevitable; and the world will soon resolve itself into the semblance of an ant hill, governed by commissars who owe their power to the profundity of their contempt for the individual members of their species." The point I was trying to make all through "Idiot's

Delight" is the same point that I have tried again
to make in the radio speech by Doctor Valkonen
in the first scene of "There Shall Be No Night."

Just half way between the writing of these two
plays, in 1937, I wrote "Abe Lincoln in Illinois."
That was a logical development, although I wasn't
aware of it at the time. It was the story of a man
of peace who had to face the issue of appeasement
or war. He faced it. His "House Divided" speech
made him a national figure and the candidate of
the party which was determined to end slavery.
Douglas accused Lincoln of "inflammatory per-
suasion," of "stimulating the passions of men to
violence," but Lincoln did not retreat from the
uncompromising stand which, after years of doubt
and hesitancy, he had chosen to take. A few days
after his inauguration as President, he was con-
fronted with the grave situation of Fort Sumter.
He asked his cabinet whether in their opinion he
should send relief to Fort Sumter. The cabinet
voted eight to one against doing so, on the ground
that such action would most certainly mean war.
Lincoln, on his own authority, ordered the relief
to be sent to Fort Sumter. It did mean war—and
for Lincoln it meant four years of anguish and
then violent death. But it saved the Union.

The development of Lincoln's attitude in the
years before the Civil War paralleled the development of the attitude of the whole American people
in the years before 1940. Lincoln knew that slavery was an evil, but considered war a greater

evil. He served in Congress for one term during the Mexican War, and in 1848 he denounced that war, calling it a land grab, as indeed it was. His "unpatriotic" stand at this time caused a newspaper in his own home state to denounce him as "a second Benedict Arnold."

Lincoln then believed that, if the Southern States wanted slavery, they were perfectly free to have slavery. He didn't say much about this vital issue; but when he talked at all, he expressed his disapproval of the rabble-rousing agitations of the Abolitionists. This was the liberal democratic point of view of "live and let live." It was the point of view of ordinary Americans—and Englishmen and Frenchmen, as well—in 1936 when they said, "If the Germans want Naziism, or the Italians Fascism, or the Russians Communism, that is their business, and not ours." (I tried to say in "Idiot's Delight" that it was everybody's business. There is no more dangerous error of foreign policy than for the government of one nation to say, "We are not concerned with the internal affairs of other nations.")

It was when Lincoln saw that the spirit of acceptance of slavery was spreading—from Missouri into Kansas and Nebraska and on across the plains and mountains to Oregon and California—it was then that he turned from an appeaser into a fighter.

While "Abe Lincoln in Illinois" was in rehearsal, in September, 1938, the Munich crisis

occurred. I showed Raymond Massey a passage
from Lincoln's Peoria speech, of 1854, which
seemed to have a direct bearing on the current
situation. We decided to incorporate this into
the speech which Mr. Massey delivered so bril-
liantly in the debate scene.

Lincoln, in this passage, was talking of the
Douglas policy of "mind your own business"—the
policy of indifference to evil—the policy of appeasement. He said he "could not but hate" it.
"I hate it because of the monstrous injustice of
slavery itself. I hate it because it deprives our
republic of its just influence in the world; enables
the enemies of free institutions everywhere to
taunt us as hypocrites; causes the real friends of
freedom to doubt our sincerity; and especially
because it forces so many good men among ourselves into an open war with the very fundamen-
tals of civil liberty, denying the good faith of the
Declaration of Independence, and insisting that
there is no right principle of action but *self-
interest*."

Those words have had a profound influence on
my own thinking, or attempts at thought.

After "Abe Lincoln in Illinois," two years
passed during which I had many doubts that I
should ever write another play. I wanted to write
about that which was uppermost in my own mind
and in the minds of most other men who were still
free to speak. But how could any play hope to
compete or even keep up with the daily headlines

and the shrieks of increasing horror heard over
the radio? I said to my friend, Alexander Korda,
"I wish I could write a sparkling drawing-room
comedy without a suggestion of international calamity or social significance or anything else of
immediate importance." He laughed and said,
"Go ahead and write that comedy—and you'll find
that international calamity and social significance
are right there, in the drawing room."

With the outbreak of the second World War
in 1939 I was in a frenzy of uncertainty. I knew
all the arguments for keeping my own country
out of the European conflict; I had uttered many
of them myself, and at the top of my lungs. I had
learned that the forces which had got us into war
in 1917 were sympathy for the Allies and hatred
of German militarism, economic involvement with
the Allies, and the great national campaign for
preparedness which began at Plattsburg in 1915–
16. (I was there.) I believed that he that taketh
up the sword is going to use it, however he may
try to persuade himself, "I do this not because of
a desire to fight but because I wish to avoid fighting." That is why, for the twenty years which
followed 1918, I was a passionate advocate of
disarmament. It was a bitter moment for me when
I found myself on the same side as the Big Navy
enthusiasts.

All of these considerations were storming
around in my mind in September, 1939, and
storming with them was the conviction that Hit-

lerism was as great a menace to the United States
as it was to any free country of Europe—that as
a force it was far more formidable than most complacent people in the democracies supposed—that
England and France, if we failed to help them,
might crumble quickly before it and that then
we should be helpless to oppose it.

Being myself so confused, I couldn't speak up
with any positive conviction. I was terrified of
identifying myself as a "Warmonger." But my
mind was settled principally by two events: the
first was a speech in October by Colonel Charles
A. Lindbergh, which proved that Hitlerism was
already powerfully and persuasively represented
in our own midst; the second was the Soviet invasion of Finland.

Like many another who hopes that he is a Liberal, I had great faith in the Soviet Union as a
force for world peace. I believed it was the mighti-
est opponent of Fascism. The Russian aid to the
Spanish Loyalists and the Chinese substantiated
that belief. Even after the news of the Nazi-Soviet
treaty I continued to think wishfully that Stalin
was playing his own shrewd game against Fascism. But with the assault on Finland the last
scales of illusion fell. I knew that this was merely
part of Hitler's game of world revolution; and
it was not proletarian revolution—far from it;
it was a new and immeasurably more virulent form
of imperialism. The Soviet government was playing the old, inhuman game of power politics with

the same Machiavellian cynicism which has been Fascism's deadliest weapon against the gullible democracies. The Marxian principles of internationalism were as dead as Lenin. The Soviet warlords cared no more for the fate of the workers in the United States than they had cared for the fate of the workers in France. The sole purpose of their propaganda in the United States, as it had been in France, was to spread confusion and disunion, to weaken American resistance so that we would provide an irresistible temptation to Hitler to continue his conquests westward.

The reluctance of the United States to give help to Finland shocked me. The sentiment of our people for the Finns was obvious. Here was a decent little democracy, which had paid its debts and played no part in any of the vicious European intrigues, ruthlessly assaulted by an overwhelmingly superior force and gallantly fighting for its own freedom. There could be only one reason for America's reluctance to give any help to the Finns, and that was abject fear. And if we were in a state of abject fear, then we had already been conquered by the masters of the Slave states and we must surrender our birthright.

So I decided to raise my voice in protest against the hysterical escapism, the Pontius Pilate retreat from decision, which dominated American thinking and, despite all the warnings of the President of the United States and the Secretary of State, pointed our foreign policy toward suicidal isolationism. I wrote this play in January and February, 1940, under constant pressure of the knowledge that it might at any moment be rendered hopelessly out of date. As it happened, the war in Finland ended while the play was in rehearsal. But the story of the Finns' three months of resistance continued to be the story of all decent, civilized people who choose to stand up and fight for their freedom against the forces of atavistic despotism. Shortly after the play's first opening, two more innocent countries, Denmark and Norway, were invaded by the Nazis. Then came the invasion and conquest of Holland, Belgium and France.

I was rather surprised, under the circumstances of writing, that this play developed a spirit of optimism along toward the end. But, in expressing my own essential faith, as I have tried to do herein, I couldn't very well keep optimism out. I believe every word that Doctor Valkonen utters in the sixth scene of "There Shall Be No Night." I believe that man, in his new-found consciousness, can find the means of his redemption. We are conscious of our past failures. We are conscious of our present perils. We must be conscious of our limitless future opportunities. We are armed with more bitter experience, more profound knowledge, than any generations that ever were in the history of the world. If we can't use this experience and this knowledge then the human story is really finished and we can go back and achieve forgetfulness and peace in the ooze from which we ascended.

It seems to me, as this Preface is written, that Doctor Valkonen's pessimism concerning man's mechanical defenses and his optimistic faith in man himself have been justified by events. The Mannerheim and Maginot Lines have gone. But the individual human spirit still lives and resists in the tortured streets of London.

I wish to express my gratitude to my family doctor, Charles Goodman Taylor, for the advice he gave me in forming the scientific philosophy of Doctor Valkonen; to W. L. White, for his broadcasts over C. B. S. from Finland—especially the deeply stirring one on Christmas Day, 1939—from which I gained almost all of my sketchy knowledge of the Soviet-Finnish War; to Anne Morrow Lindbergh, for an article of hers in the January, 1940, issue of the *Reader's Digest*; to my associates of the Playwrights' Company for invaluable suggestions for revisions in this hastily written play; and—for the third time in my life—to Lynn Fontanne and Alfred Lunt.

R. E. S.

September 13th, 1940

THERE SHALL BE NO NIGHT

SCENE I

The scene is the living room of the Valkonen house in the suburbs of Helsinki. It is afternoon of a day early in October, 1938.

This is a nice, neat, old-fashioned house, with large windows, through which one sees a lovely view of the harbor and the islands.

The room is comfortably furnished. On the walls, surprisingly, are pictures from an American house. The most prominent is a portrait of a handsome naval officer of the 1812 era. There are a dismal portrait of a substantial magnate of the 1880's, and a number of pallid little water-colors of Louisiana scenes. There is a charcoal drawing of a wistful looking gentleman. On the piano and on the tables are many photographs of famous doctors—Pavlov, Freud, the Mayos, Carrel, etc.

Up-stage, a large door leads into the dining room. An unseen door leads from this into the kitchen, to the right.

The main entrance, leading from the front hall, is lower right. The piano is upper left.

Near the center of the stage is a sofa, and in front of it, on a table, are a radio microphone and a telephone.

Wire connections for this equipment run out into

1

the dining room, where there are a mixer and other equipment.

Standing at the left of this table is DR. KAARLO VALKONEN. *He is between forty-five and fifty years old—gentle, amused, vague, and now rather self-conscious. Beside him stands his wife,* MIRANDA, *who is beautiful, chic, and enjoying the whole situation intensely.* KAARLO *is a native Finn;* MIRANDA *comes from New Bedford, Massachusetts.*

In the foreground are two PHOTOGRAPHERS *with flash cameras. They are taking pictures of the Valkonens.*

Toward the right stands DAVE CORWEEN, *an American, about thirty-five years old, formerly a newspaper foreign correspondent, now a European representative of the Columbia Broadcasting System.*

FIRST CAMERA MAN

Now—Doctor——

KAARLO

Yes—I'm ready.

MIRANDA

Wait a minute——
(*She removes* KAARLO'S *glasses.*)

FIRST CAMERA MAN

Smile, please——
(*They both smile. The picture is taken. The* CAMERA MEN *bow and cross to the left.*)

DAVE

Will you both sit down, please?
(KAARLO *and* MIRANDA *sit on the sofa.*)
Dr. Valkonen, would you look as though you were talking into the mike?

KAARLO

Talking?

MIRANDA

Just say something, Kaarlo—something thrilling and profound.

DAVE

Say 1–2–3–4–5–6–7—anything.

MIRANDA

And I'll look as if I were listening, fascinated.

DAVE (*smiles*)

That's right, Mrs. Valkonen.

FIRST CAMERA MAN

Ready?
(*They pose for an instant while he takes the picture. He changes negatives and takes several more pictures during* KAARLO'S *speech.*)

DAVE

Can't you think of something? We want to test the microphone.

KAARLO (*nodding*)

Yes! I can think of something. (*He leans toward the microphone.*) How do you do, my dear friends in America? How are you? I am well. I hope you are likewise. And do you know that the human digestive tract or alimentary canal extends for a distance of twenty-five to thirty feet, and consists of the following main parts: the mouth, pharynx, œsophagus, stomach, small intestines, cæcum, large intestines, rectum and anus? Into this canal flow the secretions of the salivary glands, liver and pancreas. Don't I speak English nicely? Yes. Thank you. Is that enough?

(*The* CAMERA MEN *have finished and pack their equipment, preparing to leave.*)

DAVE

That was splendid, Doctor. Thank you very much.

SECOND CAMERA MAN

Thank you, Doctor.

KAARLO

Don't mention it, gentlemen.

MIRANDA

Will we get copies of those pictures?

FIRST CAMERA MAN

Oh yes, Mrs. Valkonen. We hope you will like them.

KAARLO

Thank you.

(*The* CAMERA MEN *bow and go out at the right.*)

DAVE (*calling toward the dining room*)
How was it, Gus?

(GUS *appears in the dining-room door. He is a young American radio mechanic.*)

GUS

It sounded fine. Just speak in that same natural way, Doctor.

(MIRANDA *turns to* DAVE *with some alarm.*)

MIRANDA

Was that radio on when he was talking?
(GUS *goes.*)

DAVE

Don't worry, Mrs. Valkonen. It was just a test. The voice went no farther than the next room.

MIRANDA

Now, Kaarlo—when you do speak to the American people, please don't forget yourself and go through all those disgusting organs again. People don't like to be reminded of such things.

KAARLO

But I don't know yet what I'm supposed to say. You haven't finished correcting that translation.

MIRANDA (*rising*)

I'll finish it now. Would you like a drink, Mr. Corween?

DAVE

Not just now, thank you.

MIRANDA

We'll all have a drink after the broadcast.

(*She goes out.* KAARLO *has been looking at the radio apparatus.*)

KAARLO

Wonderful business, this.

DAVE

Wonderful—and awful.

KAARLO

More complicated than the alimentary canal, eh?

DAVE

Perhaps. But less essential.

KAARLO

How does my voice get from here all the way to America? Can you explain that to me?

DAVE

No, Doctor—I can't. But I can give you the outline. The voice travels from the microphone along that wire into the next room. It goes into that box in there. That's called the mixer. From there, it goes over your own telephone line to the broadcasting station, where various things happen that I don't understand. It's then transmitted on another line under the Gulf of Finland to Geneva, where it's broadcast by short wave from the League of Nations station.

KAARLO

Really! So that's what the League of Nations is doing!

DAVE

Well, they've got to do something. They send your voice to some place on Long Island, where it's transmitted to C.B.S. in New York, and then re-broadcast from coast to coast.

KAARLO

My word! Do you think any one will listen?

DAVE (*laughing*)

Certainly. They'll listen to all sorts of strange things on Sunday.

KAARLO

I knew I should never have agreed to this non-sense. I'll make a fool of myself.

DAVE

Oh, please, Doctor—I didn't mean to suggest that——

KAARLO

I know you didn't. But I'm still sorry. My wife's relatives will be listening, and they will write to her and say, "Kaarlo sounds older." They live in New Bedford, Massachusetts. Have you ever been there?

DAVE

I couldn't be sure.

KAARLO

A depressing place. But good people. Terrifying—but good. All of these paintings on the wall came from the house in New Bedford. (*He points to the 1812 officer.*) There's a fine looking fellow. They must have been gayer in those days. But look at that one over there. Miranda's grandfather. Did you ever see such a brigand? That's a drawing of her father on the piano. A very sensitive face. He didn't come from New Bedford—Louisiana, I think. He painted all those watercolors—swamps, and things. Miranda loved him. He must have been very charming. But he was surely a very bad painter.

(UNCLE WALDEMAR *comes in from the right. He is a moody, disenchanted old man.* KAARLO *rises and crosses to him.*)

Ah, Uncle Waldemar—I was afraid you were going to be late. (KAARLO *kisses* UNCLE WALDEMAR.) This is Mr. Corween, of the American radio—my uncle Mr. Sederstrum.

DAVE

How do you do?

UNCLE WALDEMAR (*curtly*)

How do you do? (*He crosses to his easy chair at the left.*)

KAARLO

If you would like to have some music with the broadcast, Uncle Waldemar will play. A great

musician. He plays the organ in the Agricola
Church.

UNCLE WALDEMAR

Thank you. But I think you can do without
music.

KAARLO

Look at this machine, Uncle Waldemar. (KAAR-
LO *goes up to the couch and points to the microphone.*) My voice goes in there, and then into the
dining room where it gets mixed, and then to the
League of Nations, and then all over America.
They will all be listening, because it's Sunday. (*He
turns to* DAVE.) Will they hear me even in Minnesota?

DAVE

Yes, Doctor. Even in Minnesota.

KAARLO

It makes one frightened. (*He sits down.*)

DAVE

I know it does. I've been broadcasting for
nearly a year now, all over Europe, and I still get
mike fright when I hear that summons, "Come in,
Vienna" or "Go ahead, Prague," or wherever I
happen to be. (DAVE *sits down.*)

KAARLO

You were in Prague during the crisis?

DAVE

Yes—I just came from there—Prague and
Munich.

KAARLO

You saw all of it, there in Munich?

DAVE

As much as we were allowed to see.

KAARLO

When we read our papers the day after that meeting last week—we just couldn't believe it. Something had happened that we couldn't understand. Could we, Uncle Waldemar?

UNCLE WALDEMAR

I could. I knew it would be a disaster.

KAARLO

Uncle Waldemar always looks on the dark side of things. There's been too much Sibelius in his life.

UNCLE WALDEMAR

I can understand what happened at Munich because I know Germany. I've lived there—I've studied music there—I've read Goethe. He knew his own people. He stood on the heights, and he said that from his point of view all life looks like some malignant disease.

DAVE

Well, he should see it now. I can tell you I was glad when they ordered me to come up here. You don't know what it means to be in a really free country again. To read newspapers that print *news*—to sit around cafes and hear people openly criticizing their government. Why—when I saw a

girl in the street who wasn't afraid to use lipstick,
I wanted to go right up and kiss her.

KAARLO

Why didn't you? She'd have been very flattered.
Our girls here like Americans, especially those gay
young college boys who come here on tours——

(MIRANDA *enters with the manuscript of the
speech.* DAVE *and* KAARLO *rise.*)

MIRANDA

Here's your speech, Kaarlo. (*She gives him
his speech and crosses to* UNCLE WALDEMAR, *kissing him.*) Hello, Uncle Waldemar. I'm sorry I
missed church today, but there's been so much ex-
citement around——

UNCLE WALDEMAR

It was just the same as always.

MIRANDA (*crossing back to the table*)

Kaarlo, you'd better read that speech all over
to yourself first.

KAARLO

I'll go to our room and read it to the mirror.
(*He goes out at the right.*)

DAVE

Dr. Valkonen showed me your family portraits.

MIRANDA

Oh, did he? Did he tell you his idea—that they
represent the whole cycle of modern history? Rugged heroism—that's him—developing into ruthless
materialism—that's him— (*She has pointed first to*

the 1812 ancestor, then the 1880 one. Then she crosses to the piano and picks up the drawing.)
—and then degenerating into intellectual impotence and decay—that's him. (*She holds the picture fondly.*) Rugged heroism—that's old great-grandfather Eustis—he fought in the navy in the war of 1812.

DAVE

Did he?

MIRANDA

Yes—and he lived to sail a clipper ship to California in the Gold Rush. He didn't get any gold, but he died happy. His son, my sainted grandfather—that's that one with the beard—bought his way out of the Civil War for three hundred dollars. Then he made a nice fortune selling shoddy uniforms to the army. He did even better after the war when he packed his carpet bag and went south. He married a beautiful daughter of the ruined aristocracy, and my father was the result. (*She holds out the drawing.*) You can see he was more New Orleans than New Bedford.

(DAVE *looks at the picture over her shoulder.*) Sargent drew that. Fine drawing, isn't it?

DAVE

Superb.

MIRANDA (*crossing to the piano and replacing the drawing*)

Father avenged the honor of the Old South. When he came into possession of the family fortune, he went systematically to work and threw it away, squandered every penny that old whiskers there had scrounged and saved. And he had a wonderful time doing it. (*She gets a cigarette from a box on the piano and sits down.*) He was the idol of all the head waiters in London, Paris, Monte Carlo, Vienna. He took me along with him on his travels. He used to say to me, "Mandy, this won't last forever, but while it does, we're certainly going to make the most of it."

DAVE

And how did you happen to meet Dr. Valkonen? (*He lights her cigarette.*)

UNCLE WALDEMAR (*amused*)

Are you going to put all this on the radio?

DAVE

Oh, no! But I'd like to write something about this visit. I try to maintain my status as a newspaper man against the day when the public will get tired of being fed through their ears.

MIRANDA

Well, Kaarlo and I met in Russia in 1914. That was when my father was coming to the end of his brilliant career as a spendthrift. Kaarlo was a medical officer in St. Petersburg—that's what they called it then. Oh, he was so handsome! Thin—

dark—tragic looking. I was seventeen—I'd never seen any one like him. Of course he didn't know I was alive. Then came the war and we had to leave for America. It was the end of the world for me. I pestered him with letters regularly, and he replied—once. After the revolution, he came to America to study, and we met again, and after considerable effort on my part, we were married. And that's all there is to that.

Uncle Waldemar

Then he brought her back here, his American wife, and we asked him, "Is she rich?" and he said, "No." So we said, "Kaarlo is a fool."

Miranda

I've told you it wasn't his fault—he was too polite to refuse. (*She turns to* Dave.) All that was a long time ago. I think Uncle Waldemar has forgiven me now.

Dave

I hope I'll have the pleasure of meeting your son, Mrs. Valkonen.

Miranda

Oh, I hope so. We're expecting him any minute. He's been away on a holiday—working. They spend all their holidays in this country working. You've never seen such energetic people.

Dave

I suppose your son is completely a Finn—not an American?

MIRANDA

He can't quite make up his mind what he is. But now he has his first girl friend. She'll probably settle the matter for him.

(KAARLO *comes in, carrying his speech.*)

KAARLO

Well, I've gone through this, and I must say it seems too dull, even for Sunday.

DAVE (*looking at his watch*)

It's pretty near time. I'll see if the connection is set.

(DAVE *goes into the dining room.* MIRANDA *rises and goes down to* UNCLE WALDEMAR. *She arranges the shawl on his lap.* KAARLO *paces up and down, reading his speech.*)

MIRANDA

How's the rheumatism, Uncle Waldemar?

UNCLE WALDEMAR

It's bad.

MIRANDA

Haven't those treatments done you any good?

UNCLE WALDEMAR

No.

MIRANDA

Never mind. We'll be going soon to Italy for a holiday and we'll take you. That will make you well.

(DAVE *returns and sits at the table, arranging his introductory speech.*)

UNCLE WALDEMAR

Yes—I know what those holidays are like, in Italy, or anywhere else. All Kaarlo does is visit lunatic asylums.

(DAVE *picks up the telephone, and looks toward* GUS *in the dining room.*)

GUS'S VOICE (*from the dining room*)

Go ahead.

DAVE (*into the telephone*)

Hello—hello. This is Dave Corween—Dave Corween. . . . Hello, Ed. How's everything? . . . Yes—I got here this morning. Beautiful place— lovely people—and what a relief. . . . Yes!! . . . No—I don't see how there can possibly be *another* crisis this year. . . . Maybe they'll let me come home for Christmas. . . . No—it's wonderfully quiet up here. Sweden, too. Yes—I came through Stockholm yesterday. (*To* KAARLO *and* MIRANDA.) If you'll sit down, we're about ready.

(*They sit on the sofa by the table.*)
How's the world series? . . . They did, eh. . . . Yes—I'm watching the time. 43½—O.K. (*He looks at his watch.*) . . . Good-bye, Ed.

MIRANDA (*to* KAARLO)

Good luck, darling—and just remember—it doesn't really matter.

Gus's Voice (*from the dining room*)
O.K., Dave.

DAVE

Listen!

VOICE FROM LOUD-SPEAKER

This is Station WABC in New York.

KAARLO

Great God!

MIRANDA

Did you hear that, Uncle Waldemar? It's New York!

UNCLE WALDEMAR

I heard.

(DAVE *cautions them to silence.*)

VOICE FROM LOUD-SPEAKER

We now take you to the Finnish capital. Go ahead, Helsinki.

(DAVE *speaks briskly into the microphone, using notes typed on copy paper.*)

DAVE

Hello America—this is David Corween, in Helsinki. We're bringing you the first of a series of broadcasts from Finland, Sweden and Norway, those little countries in the far north of Europe which are at peace, and intend to remain at peace. Finland is a country with a population about equal to that of Brooklyn. Like many other small nations, it achieved its freedom twenty years ago—but, unlike some of the others, it has consolidated that freedom; it has made democracy work. It has no minority problems. Its frontiers are disputed by no one. Its people are rugged, honest, self-respecting and civilized.

(KAARLO *and* MIRANDA *start to speak to one another.* DAVE *signals them to be quiet and goes right on.*)

I am now speaking from the home of one of Finland's most distinguished citizens, Dr. Kaarlo Valkonen, the eminent neurologist, who has received high honors in the United States, England, the Soviet Union and other nations, and has just been awarded the Nobel Prize in medicine. In announcement of this award, the directors of the Caroline Medical Institute in Stockholm stated that Dr. Valkonen has given to mankind a new understanding of the true nature and the causes of mental diseases—and I might add that those of us who have to cover the European scene these days can appreciate how much this understanding is needed.

(KAARLO *is embarrassed and pained by all this; he keeps looking at* MIRANDA, *who, however, is delighted.*)

Many of you have read his book, *The Defense of Man,* and to some of you now listening he is known personally, as he has lived much in America, and his wife comes from that fine old Massachusetts town, New Bedford. It gives me great pleasure to bring you an outstanding servant of humanity— Dr. Kaarlo Valkonen.

(He moves the microphone over to KAARLO *and gestures to him to begin.* MIRANDA *listens intently, waiting for mishaps.)*

KAARLO *(loudly)*

I never heard so much introduction.

*(*DAVE *moves the microphone back from* KAARLO *and signals him to speak more quietly.)*

To tell the truth, I think the Nobel prize is premature. The work I am doing will be finished by some one else many years from now. But still—I am glad to have that prize, as it enables us to go for a holiday in France and Italy, and my wife will buy some new clothes in Paris.

MIRANDA

Read what is written!

*(*KAARLO *looks for the first time at his manuscript.)*

KAARLO *(reading)*

Dr. Carrel has said, "For the first time in history, a crumbling civilization is capable of discerning the causes of its decay. For the first time it has at its disposal the gigantic strength of science." And he asks, "Will we utilize this knowledge and this power?" That's a question far more important than speculating about the possible results of the Munich crisis. In fact, behind this question are the real causes of all the problems we now must face.

It is no doubt well known to you that insanity is increasing at an alarming rate. Indeed, the day is within sight when the few remaining sane people are put into confinement and the lunatics are at large.

Does this seem a ridiculous exaggeration? Then look about you, at the present world. You see the spectacle of a great, brilliant nation, which has contributed perhaps more than all others to scientific progress. Today, the spiritual resistance of its people has been lowered to such an extent that they are willing to discard all their moral sense, all the essential principles of justice and civilization. They glorify a theory of government which is no more than co-ordinated barbarism, under the leadership of a megalomaniac who belongs in a psychopathic ward rather than a chancellery. He seeks to create a race of moral cretins whom science has rendered strong and germless in their bodies, but feeble and servile in their minds. We now know how quickly such men can be converted into brutes.

It is all very well to say, "We will go to war and crush this mighty force. Free men will always triumph over slaves." But after the war—and on into the centuries—what then? How long will these same free men possess the spiritual strength that enables them to be free? There is a problem for science to solve—and we must begin by admitting our own mistakes.

Science has considered disease as mechanical phenomena, to be cured by mechanical means. And we have been remarkably successful. Examine the achievements in the fight against tuberculosis—

typhoid—all the ancient plagues. You will see that the number of fatalities is steadily being reduced. Then look at the degenerative diseases—insanity, which is the degeneration of the brain—and cancer, which is degeneration of the tissues. These diseases are going up, almost in the same proportion as the others are going down.

Degeneration! That is the most terrifying word in the human vocabulary today. And doctors are beginning to ask, "Is there not a suspicious connection between our victories and our defeats? Are we perhaps saving children from measles and mumps that they may grow up to be neurotics and end their days in a mad-house?" Perhaps their early battles with disease toughen them. Perhaps without that essential experience, they go into maturity without having developed adequate defenses against life. What are these defenses?

St. Paul has said: "We glory in tribulation; knowing that tribulation worketh patience; and patience, experience; and experience, hope." We have been striving to eliminate tribulation, and as we have succeeded we have deprived man of his experience, and thus of his hope.

We have counted too heavily upon pills and serums to protect us from our enemies, just as we count too heavily upon vast systems of concrete fortifications and big navies to guard our frontiers. Of what avail are these artificial protections if each man lacks the power of resistance within himself?

I am not pleading for a return of measles and mumps. I am only saying that all of us have been trying too hard to find the easy way out—when man, to *be* man, needs the experience of the hard way. "There is no coming to consciousness without pain," in the words of Dr. Jung, and Science has provided no substitute for pain.

You have heard it said that the days of exploration are over—that there are no more lost continents—no more Eldorados. But I promise you that the greatest of all adventures in exploration is still before us—the exploration of man himself—his mind—his spirit—the thing we call his character —the quality which has raised him above the beasts.

"Know thyself," said the oracle. And after thousands of years, we still don't know. Can we learn before it is too late—before the process of man's degeneration has been completed and he is again a witless ape, groping his way back into the jungle? (*He looks up and thrusts his manuscript away.*) But why should I go on spoiling your Sunday? I want to send my greetings to New Bedford, Massachusetts. I want to send especial greetings to Minnesota, home of my dear good friends, the Mayos. Perhaps I have an especial feeling of love for Minnesota because it is so much like Finland, with many beautiful lakes, and forests of birch and pine and spruce. And I know so many fine people there, with good blood that came from Finland, and our neighboring countries of Sweden, Norway and Denmark.

To them, and to all my friends in the United States
of America I say, "Thank you and God bless you
and good-bye."

(*He turns to* MIRANDA *and shrugs as though to
say,* "*I'm sorry but that was the best I could do.*"
MIRANDA *leans over and kisses him.*)

DAVE (*into the microphone*)

Thank you, Dr. Kaarlo Valkonen. This is David
Corween in Helsinki, returning you now to Columbia in New York.

KAARLO	VOICE FROM LOUD-SPEAKER
Never will I speak to one of those damned things again.	We take you now to London. . . .

MIRANDA (*rising*)

Darling—you were wonderful! Didn't you think
it was fine, Uncle Waldemar?

UNCLE WALDEMAR

If they'll listen to that, they'll listen to anything.

DAVE (*rising*)

You were splendid, Doctor. A definite radio
personality.

MIRANDA

There!

KAARLO (*pleased*)

You really think so?

(GUS *comes in from the dining room to clear the
table of equipment.*)

MIRANDA

Of course he does. Now I'll go and mix the drinks. (*She goes off into the dining room.*)

GUS

They said it came through fine. I liked it myself. And I'm going to get that book of yours, Doctor. I probably can't understand it—but I'll bet it's good.

KAARLO

Why—thank you—thank you.

(GUS *goes out into the dining room.*)

What a charming man!

DAVE

I read your book last summer when I was resting between crises. And just the other day, when I heard I was coming up here about the Nobel Prize, I tried to get a copy in Munich. The bookseller assured me, solemnly, that there could be no such book, since he had never heard of it.

KAARLO (*rising*)

Of course, all my books are forbidden in Germany. I should be ashamed of myself if they weren't.

(ERIK VALKONEN *comes in from the right. He is seventeen years old, but mature and calm. He is handsome and healthy; there is a kind of quiet humor in his expression. With him is his girl friend,* KAATRI ALQUIST, *young, pretty, also healthy, and quite serious. Each of them carries a package.* KAARLO *goes immediately to* ERIK, *kisses him.*)

Erik! You're just too late for my broadcast. You missed something wonderful. Hello, Kaatri, my dear.

(KAATRI *curtsies to* KAARLO. ERIK *hands* KAARLO *his package.*)

ERIK

I brought you this from Viipuri, Father.

KAARLO

Viipurin Rinkelia! I'll have it with my coffee. (*He takes* KAATRI *over to* DAVE.) Let me introduce Miss Kaatri Alquist, Mr. Corween of the American radio. And my son, Erik.

(KAATRI *curtsies to* DAVE *and crosses to* UNCLE WALDEMAR. *After greeting her,* UNCLE WALDEMAR *points toward the dining room, as* ERIK *and* DAVE *shake hands.*)

ERIK AND DAVE

How do you do?

UNCLE WALDEMAR

Mrs. Valkonen is in the dining room.

(KAATRI *goes into the dining room.* ERIK *crosses to* UNCLE WALDEMAR.)

KAATRI'S VOICE

Hello, Mrs. Valkonen.

MIRANDA'S VOICE

Kaatri, how lovely!

ERIK (*kissing* UNCLE WALDEMAR)

Father says he was wonderful on the radio. Is that true?

UNCLE WALDEMAR

He only said the same things you've heard a hundred times before.

KAARLO

Erik, take this to your mother in the dining room.

(ERIK *takes the package from* KAARLO *and goes into the dining room.*)

ERIK

Mother! Mother! I'm back!

MIRANDA'S VOICE

Erik, darling! Did you have a good time?

KAARLO (*proudly*)

Fine boy, isn't he, Mr. Corween?

DAVE

Yes, fine. It's a shame he didn't hear your broadcast. He'd have been proud of you.

KAARLO

Oh—I'm an object of contempt to my own son—because, while I talk, he *acts*. He has been working on the Mannerheim Line.

DAVE

I'm afraid I don't know where that is.

KAARLO

It's on the isthmus—on the Russian frontier. It's our own little Maginot.

MIRANDA (*entering from the dining room with* ERIK *and* KAATRI)

Yes, he's a definite radio personality. . . . (*She puts the box of chocolates on the piano.*) Now we're going to have some coffee, and some Parker House Punch especially for you, Mr. Corween. Go and wash, children.

KAATRI

Yes, Mrs. Valkonen.

(*The two maids,* ILMA *and* LEMPI, *come in from the dining room with tablecloth, coffee urn, and service for six which they put on the table.*)

ERIK

You're not going just yet, Mr. Corween?

DAVE

Oh, no.

ERIK

Thank you. (*He bows and goes out after* KAATRI *at the right.*)

MIRANDA (*sitting on the sofa*)

You know, whenever any one comes home, from anywhere, there has to be a present. Kaatri brought me those chocolates, and Erik brought his father some of the bread they make in Viipuri. It's the custom of the country. Charming, isn't it?

Dave

Yes. (*He starts to sit down.*)

Miranda (*under her breath*)

That's Uncle Waldemar's chair. Come and sit by me.

Dave (*sitting on the couch*)

I've noticed that here—and in Sweden, too—everybody is insufferably polite. Why, yesterday, in Stockholm, my cab side-swiped another cab, so the two drivers got out and apologized to each other. It's unnatural.

(Uncle Waldemar *sits at the coffee table.*)

Miranda

I know. I've lived here for twenty years. I've never got used to it. (*She is starting to pour the coffee.*)

Kaarlo

I used to think, Mr. Corween, in my ignorance, that you Americans have no national character. My wife has taught me my error. Her character is strong enough to resist all civilizing influences. And sometimes I think our son has inherited too much from her. (*He sits down at the table.*)

Miranda

That's what Kaatri thinks. Kaatri is the girl friend I was telling you about. I'm afraid she disapproves of me. I'm too shallow—too frivolous.

KAARLO

Oh, Kaatri comes from a typically Finnish military family. Her father is a colonel and her brothers are all brought up to be fighters. Very formidable! Maybe she does disapprove of you, my dear, but in her heart she wishes she could be more like you. She wishes she could have as much fun as we do.

MIRANDA

I'll have a good talk with her some time.

DAVE

I'm interested in that work your son is doing.

KAARLO

I tell him it's silly—but he won't listen.

DAVE

It seems a sensible thing for any one to be preparing for trouble these days.

KAARLO

Yes—eminently sensible. But they don't know how to prepare. That's the trouble. They build those concrete pillboxes, and tank traps—as if such things could save anybody when Armageddon comes.

MIRANDA

What does it matter, darling? They enjoy doing the work.

KAARLO

Yes—and I suppose it's good exercise.

(ERIK *and* KAATRI *come in and go to chairs at the left, by the piano.*)

Erik and hundreds of other students spend all their free time on the Mannerheim Line. Kaatri is there, too, with the women's organization, to do the cooking and cleaning. Oh, they have a lot of fun— and maybe a little romance in the long evenings, eh, Kaatri?

KAATRI (*she giggles, then answers soberly*)

In the evening we have discussions, Dr. Valkonen.

(ERIK *brings* KAATRI *a cup of coffee.*)

DAVE

And may I ask—what sort of things do you discuss?

KAATRI

Last night we tried to arrive at some conclusions about the consequences of the Munich treaty.

DAVE

I'd like to know what your conclusions were?

ERIK

Just what you would probably hear in a similar discussion in America, Mr. Corween. We thanked heaven for the geography which puts us so far from the scene of action. We were grateful that we do not live in Czechoslovakia, or the Balkans, or even England or France.

(LEMPI *enters with the punch.*)

MIRANDA (*looking around*)

Ah—here it is! Here's the Parker House Punch, Mr. Corween. The old Parker House bar was the first place my father headed for after the reading of the will. I can't cook anything—but I can make the best rum punch and eggnog too. If you're ever here on New Year's Day, I'll give you some eggnog.

DAVE

I shall not forget that invitation. (*He is happy to be in the midst of such an untroubled, harmonious family.*)

ERIK

You came all the way here just to have my father broadcast?

KAARLO

You see?

DAVE

I'm ordered to travel around Scandinavia and pick up as many features as I can.

MIRANDA

I think we should drink a toast—to our benefactor, the late Alfred Nobel.

(*They all rise.*)

KAARLO

That's it—Nobel!

KAARLO AND MIRANDA

God bless him!

ERIK

The dynamite king.

MIRANDA

Hush, Erik. That's not in good taste.
(UNCLE WALDEMAR *crosses and sits at the piano. The others resume their seats.*)

KAARLO

As for me, I don't care where the money came from. Two million marks—forty thousand dollars.

MIRANDA (*reverting to New England*)

To say nothing of the solid gold medal.

KAARLO

To think I should see that much in a lifetime, let alone all at once.

DAVE (*to* ERIK)

What are you studying?

ERIK

Economics—sociology.

KAARLO

And ski-ing. He can't make up his mind whether he wants to be another Karl Marx, or another Olympic champion.

DAVE

Have you been much in the Soviet Union?

ERIK

Oh, yes. We lived there when father was working with Pavlov.

DAVE

And you really believe they might invade this country?

ERIK

If there were counter revolution in Russia, anything might happen. Or the Nazis might come that way. We have to be prepared.

MIRANDA

Erik, open the chocolates. Uncle Waldemar, play something. Play something gay. This is a celebration.

UNCLE WALDEMAR

I don't feel gay.

MIRANDA

Then drink this rum punch quickly and have a few more, and you'll forget your rheumatism. (*She takes him a glass of punch.*)

DAVE

Of course, the Nazis have been highly successful in terrifying people of the Bolshevik menace. But all the times I've been in Moscow, I've never seen anything but a passionate desire to be let alone, in peace.

(UNCLE WALDEMAR *starts to play a particularly gloomy selection by Sibelius.*)

KAARLO

Certainly. I know the Russians. I was a medical officer in their army and I was with them in

prison camp in Germany all through 1916. And
during the revolution I was right there in Leningrad on the staff of the Strelka Hospital. I treated
Lenin for a sore throat! And I can tell you about
these Russians: they love to plot—but they don't
love to fight. And the reason they don't love to
fight is that they're a little like the Italians—
they're too charming—they really don't know how
to hate.

(*During the foregoing speech the doorbell has
been heard, faintly, and* LEMPI *has crossed to the
right and gone out.*)

MIRANDA

Uncle Waldemar, what is that you're playing?

UNCLE WALDEMAR

Sibelius.

MIRANDA

Oh, darling, can't you play something a little
less solemn?

(LEMPI *returns and hands* MIRANDA *a card on a
silver plate.* UNCLE WALDEMAR *stops playing.*)
What is it? Oh, it's Dr. Ziemssen. Tell him to
come in.

(LEMPI *goes out.*)

KAARLO (*rising*)

Dr. Ziemssen is a neighbor of ours.

(DR. ZIEMSSEN *comes in. He is a mild, scholarly,
correct German of thirty-five or forty.* KAARLO
meets him at the door.)
Come in, Dr. Ziemssen. I'm delighted to see you.

ZEIMSSEN (*shaking* KAARLO'*s hand*)

Herr Doktor.

(ZIEMSSEN *goes to* MIRANDA, *who rises and holds out her hand.* ZIEMSSEN *kisses it.*)

MIRANDA

How do you do, Dr. Ziemssen?

ZIEMSSEN

Frau Valkonen.

MIRANDA

You know Miss Alquist—and my family.

ZIEMSSEN (*bowing to each*)

Fräulein—Herr Sederstrum—Erik.

KAARLO

And may I introduce Mr. Corween of the American radio, Dr. Ziemssen.

ZIEMSSEN

Mr. Corween! I have heard a great deal of you.

DAVE (*sitting*)

Well—that's unusual.

KAARLO

Please——

(*Indicating a chair to* ZIEMSSEN.)

Dr. Ziemssen is the German Consul General. He has heard of everybody. (KAARLO *sits down.*)

ZIEMSSEN (*smiles*)

Only the important people. I walked over, Herr Doktor, because I just this minute talked to Berlin on the telephone and they said they had heard your broadcast. They said it came through excellently and was highly entertaining.

DAVE

It was broadcast in Germany?

ZIEMSSEN

Oh, no. But it was heard at the government shortwave station.

KAARLO

Good God! I seem to remember that I said some things that were not for your government to hear.

ZIEMSSEN

Have no worries on that score, Herr Doktor. We are well accustomed to hearing the worst about ourselves. We have heard you frequently, Mr. Corween.

KAARLO

Don't be frightened by Dr. Ziemssen. He was an anthropologist before he became a diplomat. He is very broadminded.

MIRANDA

Will you have some American punch, Dr. Ziemssen?

ZIEMSSEN

Thank you, no.

KAARLO

Then have some coffee and I'll have another cup too—and some of that Viipurin rinkelia that Erik brought.

ZIEMSSEN

Viipurin Rinkelia! (*He turns to* ERIK.) Erik
—is the work getting on well?

ERIK

It seems to be. Of course I see only a small part
of it.

ZIEMSSEN

The Finnish defenses are magnificent. No one
will dare to challenge them.

ERIK

The Czechs had fine defenses, too.

ZIEMSSEN

Ah, but you are more intelligent than the Czechs.
You have no Allies—to betray you! (*He laughs at
that pleasantry.*) How do you feel about that,
Mr. Corween? You were at Munich.

DAVE

I'm afraid I have no feeling about anything.

MIRANDA

Then have some more punch, Mr. Corween.

DAVE (*laughs*)

No, thank you. (*To* ZIEMSSEN.) If you had
asked me that question a few years ago—if you had
asked me any questions of cosmic significance—I
could have answered without a moment's hesita-
tion. I was the youngest genius ever to be given a
by-line in *The Chicago Daily News*. I was on in-

timate terms with both God and Mammon. The wisdom of the ages was set before me, on the half-shell. All I had to do was add horseradish and eat.

ZIEMSSEN (*smiles*)

You have become a little less confident in recent years?

DAVE

Well, since then I have been de-educated, if there is such a word. I've covered Manchukuo, Ethiopia, Spain, China, Austria, Czechoslovakia. And all I can say is—I'm bewildered. But I suspect, Dr. Valkonen, that when you say the human race is in danger of going insane, you're not so much a prophet of future doom as a reporter of current fact. (*He becomes conscious of the fact that he is holding the floor. He smiles.*) I seem to be sounding off. That punch is powerful.

MIRANDA

Good! Then have some more and tell us what it was like in Ethiopia.

DAVE

Thank you. I mustn't. I must try to find out what it's like here. (*To* ERIK.) Do you suppose I could get permission to visit those defenses you're working on?

ERIK

I should think so. Planes from Leningrad are flying over that region all the time, so I don't believe there's much secrecy.

Dave

I must try to get there. There might be material for a broadcast.

Kaarlo

If there's anything I can do—any letters of introduction?

Dave (*rising*)

Oh, no, thank you. I'm trained to push in anywhere. Thank you very much, Mrs. Valkonen. You've been very kind. . . .

Miranda (*shaking hands with him*)

And you've been very nice. I hope you'll come and see us again.

Dave

I'll probably be back some time. (*He crosses to shake hands with* Erik.) Certainly in 1940 for the Olympic games. Good-bye, Mr. Valkonen.

Erik

Good-bye, Mr. Corween.

Dave (*to each in turn*)

Good-bye, Miss Alquist. (*To* Uncle Waldemar.) Good-bye, sir—please don't get up. (*To* Ziemssen.) Good-bye, sir. (*He crosses to* Kaarlo.) Good-bye, Doctor——

Kaarlo

Oh, I'll see you to the door.

(*They go out at the right.* Miranda, Kaatri, *and* Ziemssen *sit.*)

Miranda

Do you like him, Erik? He's nice, isn't he?

Erik

Yes. I wish I could do work like that. To be able to wander all over the earth—and see things—without being a part of them.

(Kaatri *darts a worried look at* Erik. *She knows he is now talking with his mother's voice.*)

Kaatri (*with surprising vehemence*)

I'd hate such a life!

Miranda

Why, Kaatri?

Kaatri

When you see too much of the world it makes you cynical. I'd never want to be that.

Miranda

I shouldn't either. But I've travelled all over and it hasn't made me cynical. Perhaps that's because I'm just plain stupid.

Ziemssen

Ah no, Frau Valkonen. It is only because you are an American.

Erik

A journalist like Mr. Corween has the opportunity to see the *truth*. Maybe the ultimate truth is the ultimate futility——

MIRANDA (*laughing at this*)

Oh, dear. That boy really should have a beard.

ERIK

Even so—I'd like to know the truth about the world. All of it!

(UNCLE WALDEMAR *starts to play a gay tune.*)

MIRANDA

Kaatri, the next time we go to America, I'll ask your father and mother if you can go with us. Would you like that?

KAATRI

Oh, I think I should love that!

(KAARLO *returns and sits beside* MIRANDA.)

KAARLO

I hope some of your relatives will send us a cable so we'll know how I really sounded.

MIRANDA (*again reverting to New England*)

If I know New Bedford, they'll send a postcard. . . . What's that you're playing now, Uncle Waldemar?

(UNCLE WALDEMAR *doesn't hear. She turns to* DR. ZIEMSSEN.)
What is that?

ZIEMSSEN (*listening, appreciatively*)

I believe that is Merikantor's "Tolari Ja Huotari," isn't it? (*He listens for a moment.*) Yes— a delightful little Finnish folk song.

(UNCLE WALDEMAR *continues to play, with tinkling variations on the theme.*)

MIRANDA

Oh—I love that.

(*She pats* KAARLO's *hand. They listen silently, happily to the music.*)

CURTAIN

SCENE II

The same. An evening late in November, 1939.

KAATRI *is sitting on the couch, looking toward* ERIK, *who is at the window by the piano, looking out.* KAATRI *is crocheting.*

KAATRI

What are you looking at, Erik?

ERIK (*who obviously has to think for an instant before answering this question*)

I'm looking at the stars.

KAATRI

Oh.

ERIK

There are millions of them. They're so bright you can see them reflected on the snow.

KAATRI

I know why you're looking out the window, Erik. Many people are looking out of their windows tonight—watching for the bombers.

ERIK (*turning from the window*)

Now, Kaatri! There are no bombers coming here.

KAATRI

That's what they said in Poland. I'm sure they kept telling themselves, "The bombers won't come.

43

Something will happen. There'll be another Munich. There'll be a revloution in Germany. The United States will forbid Europe to have a war. *Something* is sure to happen to prevent the bombers from coming to Poland." But they did come.

ERIK

They were Nazis.

KAATRI

The Russians went into Poland, too.

ERIK

Yes, and why not? The Nazis had done the work. (*He comes over and sits near her.*) All the Russians had to do was march in and take all that territory at no cost to themselves. But—they know perfectly well if they attack us it would mean betrayal of the revolution! The suffering they might inflict on us would be insignificant compared to the murder of their own honor.

KAATRI

Honor!

ERIK

That's what my father says, and he knows them.

KAATRI (*putting down her crocheting*)

I don't believe they ever had any honor—Tsarists or Bolshevists either. My father knows them, too. That's why he has spent his life preparing to fight them when they invade our country.

ERIK (*laughs*)

Oh—Kaatri—don't let's sit here telling each other what our fathers say. We're old enough to make up our own minds, aren't we?

KAATRI

I don't know, Erik.

ERIK

You've made up your mind that we're going to be married, haven't you?

KAATRI

Yes. (*She laughs, shyly.*) But—that's different.

ERIK

I'm glad it *is* different. The trouble with old people is—they remember too much—old wars, old hates. They can't get those things out of their minds. But we have no such memories. We're free of such ugly things. If there's going to be a better future, we're the ones who are going to make it. (*He takes her hands.*) Kaatri——

KAATRI

Yes, Erik?

ERIK

Next summer I'll stop being a student. I'll be a worker! And you and I will be married.

KAATRI (*thrilled*)

What will we live on, Erik?

ERIK (*heroically*)

On what I make. It won't be much—but it will be enough. I'll be your man—and you'll be my woman.

(*They both draw apart, laugh, and then they kiss.*)

KAATRI

We'll have a wonderful wedding, won't we, Erik?

ERIK

Yes—I suppose our families will insist on that. (*They are still in each other's arms.*)

KAATRI

It will be in the Agricola Church, and there'll be lots of flowers.

ERIK

Your father will be looking stern and magnificent in his colonel's uniform. And my father, in his black coat, looking bored. And Mother behaving like a grand duchess, and Uncle Waldemar playing da-da-de-dum. . . . (*He hums a bar of the Wedding March.*) And then we'll escape from all of them, and go home, and have several children.

KAATRI

Erik!

(*They both laugh happily and kiss each other again.*)

ERIK

Oh, Kaatri! We'll be happy people, you and I. That's all that matters, isn't it, dearest?

KAATRI

Yes. (*Suddenly the happiness fades from her face.*) No! It isn't all that matters!

ERIK

What else is there?

KAATRI (*looking away from him, but still holding him close*)

There's *now*. . . . There's this. . . . There may be war. Next summer may never come to us.

ERIK

I tell you—we don't have to think about those things. We're young, and we're free. We have only our own love, for each other.

(UNCLE WALDEMAR *comes in. He carries a newspaper. He looks at them. They break apart guiltily, rise, and confront him with great embarrassment.*)

Oh, please forgive me, Uncle Waldemar. We were——

UNCLE WALDEMAR

Yes.

ERIK

We were only——

UNCLE WALDEMAR

I saw what you were doing. I'm sorry to have interrupted. (*He kisses* KAATRI, *then* ERIK, *and crosses to the piano.* KAATRI *sits down again.*) But there's some news here.

ERIK

What is it?

UNCLE WALDEMAR

It may be good. Our government has received a message from the United States government, from Washington. They also sent the same message to Moscow. (*He comes close to them.*) It's offering their good offices to settle the Soviet-Finnish dispute. That's what they call it—the dispute. Here's what they say.

(*As he starts to read,* ERIK *sits on the sofa beside* KAATRI.)
"We would view with extreme regret any extension of the present area of war and the consequent further deterioration of international relations." That's what they say in Washington.

KAATRI (*who is holding* ERIK's *hand*)

Do you suppose the Russians will listen to that?

ERIK

Of course they'll listen.

KAATRI

Erik believes they won't attack us. What do you believe, Uncle Waldemar?

UNCLE WALDEMAR

I know they *will!*

KAATRI (*to* ERIK)

There!

Uncle Waldemar

Do you know what the press in Moscow is saying about us? We're "that Finnish scum"—we're "bourgeois bandits"—"Tools of British imperialism"—"Fascist assassins." (*He crosses to the left and flings the newspaper onto the piano.*) Those words are the advance guard of the Red Army!

Erik

My father doesn't agree with you.

Uncle Waldemar

And what does *he* know about it?

Erik

As much as any one could. He understands the Russians. He was the good friend of Pavlov and Gorki, and even Lenin himself.

Uncle Waldemar

All those gentlemen you mention are dead. And the revolution—that's dead, too. It's embalmed and exposed in a glass coffin in front of the Kremlin. It is respected—but dead. Now comes the true disintegration—the end of the world. Your father said—men might become again like apes, groping their way back into the jungle. Well—it has come to pass. Men are groping their way through the night. The lights are out in Berlin, Paris, London. And in Warsaw, they crawl through the ruins like rats. It will be the same here. This is war in the jungle, and the winner will be crowned "King of Beasts."

(MIRANDA *comes in from the right, looking very smart in her furs and her Paris hat.* ERIK *and* KAATRI *rise.*)

ERIK

Hello, Mother. Where's Father?

MIRANDA (*taking off her hat and coat*)

He's at the laboratory. (*She puts her wraps on a chair at the right.*) I went there to try to make him come home. He had a lot of dogs there—there must have been thirty or forty of them—all barking and howling. I asked him what he was doing with all those dogs, but he told me to go away. (*She kisses* KAATRI.) Kaatri—are your mother and father well?

KAATRI

My mother is well, thank you. My father is with the army in the north.

MIRANDA

But he'll surely be home for Christmas?

KAATRI

Oh, yes, Mrs. Valkonen—we hope so.

(MIRANDA *has come up to* ERIK. *She kisses him.*)

UNCLE WALDEMAR

I have to go to the church and practice. There's to be a great service this evening—prayers for peace.

MIRANDA (*sitting down on the sofa*)

I know.

UNCLE WALDEMAR

The President will be there and the Cabinet and the leaders of all parties. (*He starts to cross toward the door at the right.*) Tonight—prayers. Tomorrow—guns. (*He goes out. There is a moment of constrained silence.*)

MIRANDA

I stopped in at the American Legation on my way home and saw Mr. Walsh. I wanted to find out if he had any news. He told me that the State Department has ordered all Americans to leave Finland at once. He was very guarded in his choice of words—but he seems to think that things are rather serious.

ERIK

So does Uncle Waldemar. But that doesn't mean anything. The American government—all governments—are being pulverized with fear by this Soviet propaganda. (*He picks up the paper from the piano.*) They want to pulverize us, too, so that we'll give them what they want without a struggle. It's all bluff—it's all an imitation of the Nazis.

KAATRI

But when the bluff doesn't work, suppose they go on imitating the Nazis—suppose they do attack?

(MIRANDA *looks from* KAATRI *to* ERIK, *awaiting his reply.*)

ERIK (*without emotion*)

Then—we'll have to fight—that's all.

MIRANDA

But—how can we fight?

ERIK

To the best of our ability.

MIRANDA

And how long will that last?

ERIK

A few days—a few weeks—I don't know. (*He is looking out the window.*)

MIRANDA

Erik—*Erik!*

(*He turns to her.*)

Would *you* fight?

ERIK

Of course I would. Everybody would!

MIRANDA

Why? What good would that do?

ERIK

It would prove that this country has a right to live.

MIRANDA

And who will derive any benefit from that proof? Are you anxious to die just to get applause from' the civilized world—applause and probably nothing else? The Czechs are fine, brave people—but they didn't offer any resistance to the Germans.

ERIK

They couldn't. Their resistance was stolen from them at Munich.

MIRANDA

Even so—they're better off now than the Poles, who did resist.

ERIK

That doesn't affect my feeling. I only know that if any one is going to take my freedom from me, he's going to have to pay for it.

MIRANDA

Now you're talking like a boy scout.

ERIK

I'm your son, Mother. I have the same blood in me that you have—the blood of that gentleman up there. (*He points to the portrait of great-grandfather Eustis.*) He fought pirates in the Mediterranean. He fought with Jackson at New Orleans.

MIRANDA

Yes—and when he died, in honored old age, they had to pass the hat around among the neighbors to get enough to bury him. . . . (*Pointing to the portrait of her grandfather.*) Whereas that unselfish hero who paid another man to take his place in the conscript army—when he died—the whole

town turned out—the Chamber of Commerce, the
Republican Club, the Knights of Pythias—all pay-
ing tribute to the memory of a good, substantial
citizen. If you have to look to your ancestry for
guidance, look to him. He was no hero. He was a
despicable, slimy cheat. But he did very well. . . .
You say some one will have to pay for your freedom. But who will receive the payment? Not you,
when you're dead.

KAATRI (*fiercely*)

Don't listen to her, Erik! Don't listen to her!

MIRANDA (*amiably*)

Why shouldn't he listen to me, Kaatri?

KAATRI (*with too much vehemence*)

Because you're an American! You don't understand.

MIRANDA (*patiently*)

I understand one thing, Kaatri. Erik is my
son. I want to save his life.

KAATRI

What good is his life if it has to be spent in
slavery? (*To* ERIK.) And that's what it would be
if he gave in to them. Slavery for you—for all of
us. Oh, I know that you Americans don't like to
think of such terrible things.

ERIK

Kaatri! You mustn't say that——

Miranda (*gently*)

You may say what you please about me, Kaatri.
But you can't say it about Erik. He's as loyal as
you are. He was born in this house, as his father
was before him.

Kaatri

Dr. Valkonen is like you. He doesn't really belong to this country. He is a great scientist. He
has an international mind.

Miranda

And is that a bad thing?

Kaatri

Oh, no—it's a good thing—a noble thing. But
for Erik—it would be weakness. I'm afraid for
Erik—afraid that he belongs more to America than
he does to us. Oh—I don't want to be rude, Mrs.
Valkonen—to you or your country. But we're desperate people now. All the men in my family—my
father, my brothers—they're all in the army now,
on the frontier. It's the same with all families,
rich and poor, men and women. All our lives we've
had to be ready to fight, for everything we are,
everything we believe in. Oh, I know—it's hard for
you to understand that—or to see the *need* for it
that is in our souls.

Erik

Kaatri! Of course Mother can understand!
Americans fought for that same thing—for the
same reason—the same need, that was in their souls.

It was Americans who taught the whole world that it was *worth* fighting for!

KAATRI

Yes. But—it's just as Dr. Valkonen says. When life becomes too easy for people, something changes in their character, something is lost. Americans now are too lucky. (*She looks straight at* MIRANDA.) In your blood is the water of those oceans that have made your country safe. But—don't try to persuade Erik that life here is as easy as it is in America. (*She is speaking passionately, desperately.*) He's a Finn, and the time has come when he must behave like one.

ERIK

Kaatri—my dearest— (*Crossing behind the sofa, he puts a hand on* KAATRI's *right shoulder. She buries her head against him.*) Don't—don't cry.

(*The word "dearest" makes an emphatic impression on* MIRANDA. *She stares at them.*)

MIRANDA

Kaatri—Kaatri—are you and Erik really in love with each other?

ERIK

Mother!

MIRANDA

Darling, I started to talk to you as though you were still a child—and I wanted first to reason with you—and then if that failed, I would *forbid* you to throw your life away for a lost cause. And then

Kaatri spoke up, and you called her "dearest," and that one word stopped me short. I asked Kaatri that question because I thought the answer might help me to understand this strange, new fact—that you're not my son any more. You're a man. . . . Of course, you don't have to answer.

ERIK (*his hand on* KAATRI's *shoulder*)
We do love each other. We are going to be married.

MIRANDA (*after a pause, kisses* KAATRI)
Erik—Kaatri—I'm glad! I'm glad.

KAARLO's VOICE (*from off-stage, right*)
Erik!
(ERIK *goes to the door.*)
Erik! You know those litters of puppies that I separated—eight litters?

ERIK
Yes, Father.

KAARLO (*entering, he throws an arm across* ERIK's *shoulders and leads him as he talks*)
The dogs have just come back from Rovaniemi—the ones I sent up there last year. The most wonderful results. I've tested them in every way. Out of thirty-one dogs, seven are definitely——

MIRANDA (*breaking in*)
Kaarlo! Kaarlo!

KAARLO

Yes, my dear. (*He slips out of his coat. To* ERIK.) Take this. (*To* MIRANDA.) I want to apologize for being a little bit irritable when you came into the laboratory—but I was excited. Those dogs. . . .

MIRANDA

Never mind about that. I have something to tell you.

(*She looks questioningly from* KAATRI *to* ERIK, *who nod permission for her to speak.*)

KAARLO (*waiting, sits*)

Yes? . . . Well?

MIRANDA

Erik and Kaatri are going to be married.

KAARLO

Erik? (*He looks at him, wonderingly, and then bursts out laughing.*)

MIRANDA (*reproachfully*)

Kaarlo!

KAARLO (*still laughing*)

Forgive me—but——

MIRANDA

Don't laugh. Now, it's not funny, Kaarlo.

KAARLO

No. No.

Miranda

No.

Kaarlo

No, I know it isn't.

Miranda

Darling—you should congratulate them at least.

Erik

Oh, let him laugh, Mother. Perhaps it *is* funny.

Kaarlo

No, no. (*Rises.*) I *do* congratulate you, Erik.
And as for you, Kaatri—
(*She rises as he goes to her*)
—you're a sweet girl and I shall be delighted to
have you for a daughter-in-law. (*He kisses her.*)

Kaatri (*curtsying*)

Thank you, Dr. Valkonen.

Kaarlo

Ever since Erik was born I've been training him
to be a gentleman of taste and discrimination, and,
by God, I've succeeded. (*To* Erik.) Again I congratulate you and thank you for justifying me.
It's really—it's unbelievable. *You*—a bridegroom!
(*He kisses him.*) But we must have some schnapps
—a toast to the happy couple. And then we will
all have supper.

Miranda

Oh darling, we're having supper later, tonight.
I told the maids they could go to church. And

we're all going to church, too. Come with us, Kaarlo. You must go and put on your tail coat.

KAARLO

And why must we all go to church?

MIRANDA

Oh, there's going to be a great service. The President and everybody will be there. We're going to pray that this country will be able to defend itself.

(KAARLO's *amusement fades instantly.*)

KAARLO

Oh! So that's it! All day I have had the utmost difficulty persuading my assistants to attend to their duties. All they wanted to think about and talk about was would we or would we not have to fight the Soviet Union? I don't want to hear any of that talk here.

MIRANDA

Neither do I, Kaarlo. But I've had to hear it. Erik is ready to fight.

KAARLO

Erik? (*He turns coldly to* ERIK.) You're a child. It seems to me that you are deciding too suddenly that you are grown up. If you want to consider yourself engaged to be married, I have no objection—I'm delighted. But I don't want to hear that you are talking to your mother, or to any one else, about going to war.

ERIK

I'm sorry, father—but I have to do what I think best.

KAARLO

And are you *able* to think?

MIRANDA

Oh, Kaarlo! Of course Erik knows——

KAARLO

No, Miranda. Don't interrupt. (*To* ERIK.) I repeat—in forming this heroic resolve to fight—have you used one grain of the intelligence that I know you possess?

ERIK

I hope I have.

KAARLO

Hoping is not good enough. You have seen those celebrations in Red Square—all those aeroplanes, those huge tanks, those troops marching—hundreds of thousands of them?

ERIK

Yes, Father—I've seen them.

KAARLO

And yet you dare to pretend you're competent to stand up against such a force as that?

ERIK

That's why I've trained with the volunteer ski troops—and why I've worked to help make the

Mannerheim Line so strong they can never break through.

KAARLO

All that nonsensical child's play on skis——

ERIK

Kaatri's brother Vaino is younger than I am—but he's with his father's regiment at the frontier . . .

KAARLO (*bitterly*)

Oh! If we are at war with the Soviet Union, *I* shall be at the frontier, too. Surely we'll need everybody, including the aged and decrepit.

MIRANDA

Now, really, Kaarlo, that is just simply ridiculous——

KAARLO (*sitting*)

I can press the trigger of a machine gun just as well as Erik. . . . So that's what we're going to pray for? Ability to imitate our enemies in the display of force. It is all nothing but a substitute for intelligent thinking.

ERIK

This is not a time for intelligent thinking! That doesn't do any good.

KAARLO

No?

ERIK

When your enemies are relying on force, you can't meet them with theories. You can't throw books at them—even good books. What else can anybody do but fight?

KAARLO (*bitterly*)

This is no time for intelligent thinking! So this is the climax of a century of scientific miracles. This is what the great men worked for—what *they* fought for in their laboratories. Pasteur, Koch, Ehrlich, Lister. They saved lives that we might build Mannerheim Lines in which to die.

(*Church bells are heard faintly in the distance.*)

MIRANDA

Now—that's enough, Kaarlo. (*Rising.*) If you don't want to go to church, you don't have to. We'll go by ourselves.

KAARLO (*rising*)

Oh, I'll put on my tail coat and go with you. I'll join in asking God to grant the impossible. But I reserve the right to say my own prayers.

(*He goes out.* MIRANDA, *who has been putting on her hat and coat, crosses to* ERIK.)

MIRANDA

We'll be ready in a few minutes. And, Erik— you must not say any more to your father about going to war.

ERIK

I'll try not to, Mother.

(MIRANDA *goes out.*)

Poor father! This is a terrible thing for him—for

a man of great faith, as he is. The rest of us
have nothing to lose but our lives.

(KAATRI *goes to* ERIK—*takes hold of him.*)

KAATRI

Erik—I love you—I do love you, and I'm sorry I
said things tonight that only made you more unhappy. I wasn't much help to you.

ERIK (*holding her tightly*)

All you said was true, Kaatri. I'm glad you
said it. I have to see things clearly. I have to see
my mother and father as they are. They don't
really live in this country—in this time. They live
together in the future—the future as my father
has imagined it—not the one that may be made by
unimaginative men. They are wonderful people—
both of them—wonderful and unreal. You *are*
real. You know what we have to face—and we will
face it without fear.

(*He kisses her, passionately.*)

KAARLO (*entering*)

This coat reeks of moth balls. It will be a
scandal in church.

MIRANDA (*offstage*)

Don't worry, Kaarlo. There'll be so much of
that smell in church they won't even notice you.
Have you a clean handkerchief?

KAARLO

Will you bring me one, please?

(ERIK *helps* KAARLO *with his coat.*)
Get your coat on, Kaatri, my dear—and you too,
Erik.

ERIK

Yes, father.

(ERIK *and* KAATRI *go out.* MIRANDA *enters, and
puts a handkerchief into* KAARLO'S *coat pocket.
He kisses her cheek.*)

KAARLO

Come, Miranda—we go to pray.

(*They start out toward the right.*)
O God, have pity, for that which we have greatly
feared has come upon us.

(*He switches off the lights. The room is in dark-
ness, except for the moonlight from the windows.
The church bells can still be heard.*)

CURTAIN

SCENE III

The same. Next afternoon.

UNCLE WALDEMAR *comes in from the right, and is surprised to see black drapes at all the windows. They are now drawn apart to let the sun in. He inspects them, goes to the piano, sits, starts to play.*

MIRANDA *calls from the dining room.*

MIRANDA'S VOICE
Uncle Waldemar!

UNCLE WALDEMAR
Yes?

MIRANDA'S VOICE
Are Kaarlo and Erik with you?

UNCLE WALDEMAR
No.

(MIRANDA *comes in from the dining room. She is wearing an apron and carrying a dust cloth.*)

MIRANDA
Have you seen them?

UNCLE WALDEMAR
I saw Kaarlo. I stopped at the hospital.

MIRANDA
Is he all right?

66

UNCLE WALDEMAR

Yes.

(*Greatly relieved, she kisses him.*)

MIRANDA

And Erik?

UNCLE WALDEMAR

Oh, I don't know anything about him. I thought he was here.

MIRANDA

I haven't seen him since the church service last night. He took Kaatri home and got in very late and then he was off this morning even before I was up.

UNCLE WALDEMAR

Probably he's with Kaatri now, at the Alquists' house.

MIRANDA

Did any bombs fall in that part of the city?

UNCLE WALDEMAR

No. I passed there on my way home. There was no damage there.

MIRANDA

Was the air raid bad?

UNCLE WALDEMAR

Not nearly as bad as expected. Maybe about thirty people killed.

MIRANDA

That's what the policeman told me.

UNCLE WALDEMAR

Were the police here?

MIRANDA

Yes, I was ordered to put up those black curtains on the windows before nightfall. There must be no light from the windows. . . . Oh, I'm so glad to see you, Uncle Waldemar. I've been alone here all day . . .

UNCLE WALDEMAR

Alone? Where are Ilma and Lempi?

MIRANDA

They're gone. They're both in the Lottas. From now on all of us will have to eat my cooking. It's three o'clock in the afternoon, and I just finished making the beds. They look frightful. . . . I wish Kaarlo and Erik would come home! What was Kaarlo doing at the hospital?

UNCLE WALDEMAR

I don't know. I saw him only for a moment. He had a white coat on.

(MIRANDA *starts dusting the furniture.*)

MIRANDA

When he left here this morning for the hospital, he said it was a good joke—his trying to be a doctor again—when it's been fifteen years since he even gave anybody an aspirin tablet.

UNCLE WALDEMAR (*coming down from the piano*)
Miranda——

MIRANDA

Yes, Uncle Waldemar.
(*She is kneeling, dusting.*)

UNCLE WALDEMAR (*with apparent difficulty*)

Miranda, I want to tell you that I am sorry for many things that I have said.

MIRANDA

What things?

UNCLE WALDEMAR

I've talked too much about the troubles of the world.

MIRANDA

And why should you feel you have to apologize for that?

UNCLE WALDEMAR

Because now I am deeply distressed.

MIRANDA

I know you are. We're all distressed. But there's nothing we can do about it.

UNCLE WALDEMAR

I have been a poor companion for you and Kaarlo. It wasn't so bad for Kaarlo because he paid no attention. But you have been so good and kind—to me and all of us here. You came here a stranger, and you made all of us love you.

MIRANDA (*harshly*)

Now, for God's sake, Uncle Waldemar, don't let's have any of that!

UNCLE WALDEMAR

But there are things on my mind, and I want to say them. You have worked so hard and so well to make this a happy home——

MIRANDA (*dusting the sofa*)

I've never done any work in my life, and I've never wanted to.

UNCLE WALDEMAR

But you have filled this house with laughter— your own peculiar American kind of laughter. And here I have been, in the midst of all this happiness, an apostle of despair.

MIRANDA

And so you want to be forgiven for telling the truth?

UNCLE WALDEMAR (*with bitter self-accusation*)

I should have had more philosophy! I—who lived for forty years under the tyranny of the Tsars— and then saw my country rise up from the ashes of the war and the revolution. I should have been reconciled to this. And you—you never saw any-thing of such real misery in your country. But now—when this came—you took it calmly. You showed wisdom.

Miranda

I took it calmly because I didn't know what was coming. I never believed it could happen. I don't believe it now. Look at me, dusting the furniture in the face of the enemy! Did you ever see such a confession of utter helplessness? (*She tosses the dust-rag aside and sits down on the sofa.*)

Uncle Waldemar

You like to believe you are merely frivolous. But you're not so foreign to us solemn Finns as you think. You're a daughter of the Puritans, who would resist any oppression, undergo any sacrifice, in order to worship God in their own way. . . . I have always believed in God's mercy. I have served Him in His church. Whenever I was in doubt and fear, I would go back to the teachings of Martin Luther—to the doctrine of "The Freedom of the Christian Man." And then I would believe again that the virtues of simple faith would always triumph over intolerance. Whenever I had enough money saved, I would go to Germany, to Eisenach, to the room in the Wartburg where Luther worked. "A mighty fortress is our God." But last year when I was there I saw the Nazis. I saw old friends of mine, living in terror—some of them because they have Jewish blood—some just because they retain a sense of common decency. Even ministers of the gospel—afraid that if they preached the true devotion to God's word they would go into concentration camps. I saw men marching—marching—marching.

(MIRANDA *rises and begins to dust again.*)

Day and night, singing "Today we own Germany—tomorrow the whole world." They didn't know where they were marching to. They didn't care. They had been drilled and lectured down to the level where marching itself was enough. I was with one of my friends, an old musician like me, and we were looking from the windows of his house. Across the street a truckload of young Nazis had pulled up and they were wrecking the home of a Jewish dentist. They wanted to take the gold he used to put in people's teeth. They were doing it systematically, as the Germans do everything. And my friend whispered to me—for he did not dare raise his voice, even in his own home—he said, "They say they are doing this to fight Bolshevism. It is a lie! For they *are* Bolshevism!" And that is the truth. . . . "Today we own Germany, tomorrow the whole world." Including Russia.

MIRANDA (*coming close to him*)

They can't win, Uncle Waldemar.

UNCLE WALDEMAR (*rises and looks out the window*)

Can *we* prevent them from winning? All we can do is defend ourselves to the end. And then they sweep over us to the next goal—and the next——

MIRANDA

You're a good Christian, Uncle Waldemar. You have to believe that they can't win.

UNCLE WALDEMAR (*passionately*)

I can believe in the coming of the anti-Christ. I can believe in the Apocalpyse. "And Satan shall be loosed out of his prison, and shall go out to deceive the nations which are in the four quarters of the earth."

(MIRANDA *dusts the keys of the piano.* ERIK *comes in at the right. He is wearing the uniform of the ski troops.*)

ERIK

Mother—I have to leave in a few minutes— (*He sees her face as she looks at him. There is a long pause.* ERIK *takes off his hat. Finally she crosses to him.*) Mother, I'm going into the north with a detachment of ski troops. I don't know just where we're being sent, but we're to assemble at the station in an hour.

MIRANDA

Is Kaatri going with you?

ERIK

No. She'll be at the station, but she doesn't know yet what they want her to do. I have to fix up my pack right away.

MIRANDA

You'll want some food for the journey. I'll get some for you. . . .

(*He kisses her cheek.*)
Whatever we have in the kitchen——

ERIK

Thank you, Mother. (*He goes out at the right.*)

MIRANDA (*to* UNCLE WALDEMAR)

If I'd only known about this sooner, I'd have gotten some things in. I—I suppose there's some canned stuff. . . . (*She seems helpless, despairing.*)

UNCLE WALDEMAR (*rising*)

I'll help you look, Miranda.

(*As they both go toward the dining room.*)
I'm sure there are plenty of good things we can find for Erik.

KAARLO'S VOICE (*from off, right*)

Miranda!

(MIRANDA *stops short.* UNCLE WALDEMAR *goes on out, into the kitchen.*)

MIRANDA

Kaarlo?

KAARLO (*entering*)

Yes. Miranda—look who has come back to Helsinki! Mr. Corween, you remember him?

(DAVE *comes in and goes to* MIRANDA.)

MIRANDA

Of course.

DAVE

I'm so glad to see you again, Mrs. Valkonen.

KAARLO

I just met him. He arrived only this morning, and he was on his way to see us. (*He goes to her and kisses her.*) It was awful, not being able to telephone?—But you're all right?

MIRANDA

Yes.

KAARLO

And Erik?

MIRANDA

Yes. He's here. He——

KAARLO

But—sit down, Mr. Corween. What will you have to drink?

MIRANDA

Kaarlo——

KAARLO (*to* DAVE)

Excuse me. Yes, my dear——

MIRANDA

Kaarlo! Erik is going into the army. He's up-stairs, now, packing his things.

KAARLO

Where is he going?

MIRANDA

I don't know. Into the north somewhere. (MIRANDA *goes to* DAVE.) Do you think there will be much fighting in the north, Mr. Corween?

DAVE

You know more about the situation than I do, Mrs. Valkonen.

MIRANDA

You'll forgive me, Mr. Corween. I have something to do.

DAVE

Of course.

(MIRANDA *goes out into the kitchen.*)
I think you'd like me to go, Dr. Valkonen.

KAARLO

No, no. Sit down, sit down. Are you going to stay here for a while in Helsinki—or is this another flying visit?

DAVE (*sitting*)

I don't know how long I shall stay. It—it all depends.

KAARLO

You'll be broadcasting from here?

DAVE

Oh, yes, Doctor. The American public likes to be kept in touch with all that's going on.

KAARLO

That's good. We like to keep in touch with them. (*He is making a gallant attempt to sustain polite conversation.*) We heard your broadcasts from Warsaw. They were brilliant.

DAVE

Thank you. I can't say I enjoyed them very much.

KAARLO (*sitting—quietly*)

It was tragic, wasn't it!

DAVE

Yes, it was. Dr. Valkonen, I know that this is no time for me to be bothering you or your wife, but——

KAARLO

You are more than welcome here, my dear friend.

DAVE

I know that, Doctor. But there's something I want to say.

KAARLO

Yes?

DAVE

I saw Jim Walsh at the American Legation.

KAARLO

Yes—yes.

DAVE

He is very fond of you and Mrs. Valkonen.

KAARLO

Thank you.

DAVE

As he should be. He asked me to beg you to leave Finland at once.

(KAARLO *looks at him.*)

He can arrange everything. A ship has been chartered next Tuesday from Goteborg, for New York. It is to take hundreds of American refugees. Mr. Walsh can arrange passage for you and Mrs. Valkonen. He can get you to Sweden by plane. But —he must know about it at once.

KAARLO

Well, now—that's very kind of Mr. Walsh, especially when he's so busy.

DAVE (*earnestly*)

I hope you will do it, Dr. Valkonen.

KAARLO

You mean—go?

DAVE

Yes—and at once.

KAARLO

I am needed here for the time being. There is a great shortage of doctors. All of the young men in all the hospitals are going to the front, for service with the army medical corps. There will be many more casualties here from air raids.

DAVE

It's not my business to say so, Doctor—but that isn't suitable work for a winner of the Nobel prize.

KAARLO (*with great sadness*)

It is not suitable work for any member of the human race, Mr. Corween. But some one must do it.

DAVE

I realize that you're a patriotic citizen of this country——

KAARLO

I am not a patriotic citizen of this country, Mr. Corween. I hope I am aware of the fact that "patriotism" as now practiced is one of the most virulent manifestations of evil.

DAVE

Yes, Doctor. That's just what I mean. You're a citizen of the world. You're of importance to the whole world, not just to these few gallant men who are going to fight and die for Finland. . . . Oh—I know it's presumptuous of me to be talking to you. But—I beg you, please, for God's sake, while you still have the chance, go to a country where you can carry on your work—your own fight —to bring men to consciousness——

KAARLO

But I shall carry on that work as long as I live, Mr. Corween—wherever I am.

DAVE

As long as you live! I'm sorry if I seem unduly emotional about it, Doctor—but—I have seen too many men of intellectual distinction forced into uniform, forced to pick up guns and shoot because they had discovered that their intelligence was impotent to cope with brutal reality. *You* may be forced into that situation, Dr. Valkonen. You who have devoted yourself to discovering the inward defenses of man. You may find yourself, crouching behind a sand-bag, shooting at an illiterate Russian peasant.

KAARLO

Yes, Mr. Corween. You know whereof you speak. And I should be the last to dispute you. Now—we feel like heroes, strong in the armor of the justice of our own cause. Soon—we may be corpses. It is all very foolish—very temporary. But, you see, I am accustomed to this sort of thing. In my youth, this country was ruled by the Romanovs. I survived that oppression. I am prepared to endure it again. Let the forces of evil engulf us. If the truth is in here, my friend——

(*He taps his heart.* MIRANDA *comes in with* ERIK.)

MIRANDA

Kaarlo, Erik must go now.

DAVE (*he knows he must get out before the possibly painful farewells are said*)

I'm afraid I must go now. (*To* ERIK.) How do you do? I—I have to get back to the hotel, to stand by for orders from New York. I'll be at the Kamp, Mrs. Valkonen, and I hope I'll see you soon again. Good-bye, Doctor. Good-bye, Mrs. Valkonen.

ERIK

Good-bye.

MIRANDA

You must come to see us often.

DAVE

Thank you, I shall. Good-bye. Good luck.

(DAVE *goes out. There is a moment of tense silence. No one knows quite what to say.*)

KAARLO (*to* ERIK)

You're leaving now?

ERIK

Yes, Father. We're to be at the station at five o'clock. I—I'd better go at once. I don't want to be late. (*To* MIRANDA.) Where's Uncle Walde-mar?

MIRANDA

He's bringing the food for you from the kitchen. You'll be able to say good-bye to him on the way out.

KAARLO

I take it you know what you're doing—what chances you have of accomplishing anything.

ERIK

Yes, Father. I think I know about that.

KAARLO

Very well, then. There's nothing I can say to you but good-bye.

ERIK (*to* KAARLO)

Father, before I go, I want you to know that I'm sorry for you. I think I understand what this is for you. It's worse for you than it is for any of us. But—if it's any consolation to you—I hope you'll remember—you have a son who at least obeys the Fourth Commandment. I honor my father and my mother.

(*The emotion of this is a bit too much for* ERIK. *He hides his face in his hands.* KAARLO *leans over and kisses him tenderly.*)

KAARLO

Go on, go on, Erik.

(ERIK *turns from him toward* MIRANDA.)

MIRANDA

I'll go to the door with you, darling.

(*They go out.* KAARLO *is alone. He goes to a chair at the extreme left, sits down, looks out the window, lost, helpless.* MIRANDA *returns and sits on the couch at the right.*)

KAARLO (*almost angrily*)

I suppose you want to weep now? Then you'd better go to our room and get it over with.

MIRANDA

What good will it do to weep? I've never in my life understood what it is to enjoy the luxury of a good cry. (*She rises suddenly.*) I'm going to the kitchen.

KAARLO

What for?

MIRANDA

I don't know. I have to start trying to learn how to cook.

(She goes out. KAARLO *looks after her misera-bly. After a moment,* UNCLE WALDEMAR *comes in.)*

UNCLE WALDEMAR

Kaarlo. . . . Kaarlo——

KAARLO

Yes.

UNCLE WALDEMAR

Dr. Ziemssen is here.

KAARLO

Dr. Ziemssen?

UNCLE WALDEMAR

He has come to say good-bye. He is going back to Germany.

KAARLO

Oh. . . . Very well, I'll see him.

UNCLE WALDEMAR (*going off at the right*)

Come in, Dr. Ziemssen.

*(*DR. ZIEMSSEN *comes in. He is wearing his over-coat, carrying his hat and walking stick.* UNCLE WALDEMAR *closes the door behind him.)*

KAARLO

I'm delighted you came in. Let me take your coat.

ZIEMSSEN

Thank you, no, Herr Doktor. I can stay but a short time.

KAARLO

Please sit down.

ZIEMSSEN

I know this is not an opportune moment. I saw
Erik go. I saluted him—a splendid young soldier.
You have good cause to be proud.

KAARLO (*as they sit on the sofa*)

Thank you, Dr. Ziemssen. I'm sorry to hear
you're going. I've greatly enjoyed our discussions
at the Institute. But—I can well understand that
this is not the place for you under the circumstances.

ZIEMSSEN (*seriously*)

It is not the place for you, either, Dr. Valkonen.
I advise you also to go.

KAARLO

Go?

ZIEMSSEN

Leave Finland. Leave Europe at once!

KAARLO

Why is everybody ordering me out of my home?
Mr. Corween was here also telling me I must leave.

ZIEMSSEN

Mr. Corween is a remarkably well-informed man.
He is aware of the inevitable outcome of this war,
as you yourself must be, Herr Doktor. Oh—I have
all admiration for the little Finnish army. But
two hundred thousand against ten million——

KAARLO

Yes, we will be conquered, as we have been conquered before. And then we will be ruled from Moscow—as we were formerly ruled from Petersburg. But as I was just saying to Mr. Corween, I shall continue with my experiments.

ZIEMSSEN

Dr. Valkonen—I must warn you—you are making a serious mistake!

KAARLO

Mistake?

ZIEMSSEN

You are judging this situation in terms of the past.

KAARLO

One can only judge by one's own experience.

ZIEMSSEN

Precisely. Your own experience is misleading.

KAARLO

In what way, Dr. Ziemssen?

ZIEMSSEN

That is just what I wish to tell you. You think our enemies are these—these Communists who now invade your country?

KAARLO

Yes. That is what I think.

ZIEMSSEN

The Russians think so, too, but they are wrong.
We are your enemies, Herr Doktor. This Finnish
incident is one little item in our vast scheme. We
make good use of our esteemed allies of the Soviet
Union. All the little communist cells, in labor
movements, youth movements, in all nations—they
are now working for *us*, although they may not
know it. Communism is a good laxative to loosen
the constricted bowels of democracy. When it has
served that purpose, it will disappear down the
sewer with the excrement that must be purged.

KAARLO

It seems to me, Dr. Ziemssen, you are talking
with extremely undiplomatic frankness.

ZIEMSSEN

I know I can do so to you, Herr Doktor. You
are a scientist. You are accustomed to face facts
—even those facts which to the ordinary, dull mind
are too terrible to contemplate.

KAARLO

What is it you are threatening, Doctor? What
is going to happen to Finland?

ZIEMSSEN

You do not know the whole story of what happened to Poland!

(KAARLO *looks at him, rises, and walks away.*)
You will hear the Pope in Rome weeping publicly

and proclaiming that the Polish nation will rise again. I assure you it will not rise again, because, as a nation, it is dead. The same is true of every nation that we conquer; we shall see to it that none of them will ever rise again. Today, the remnants of the Polish people are scattered all the way from the Rhine to the Pacific coast of Siberia. This is a process of annihilation. It is a studied technique, and it was not invented in Moscow. You will find the blueprints of it, not in *Das Kapital*, but in *Mein Kampf*. It is all there for you to read. It involves, first, liquidation of all leaders of thought —political, religious, economic, intellectual.

(KAARLO *sits down. He seems to slump.*)

Among the masses—the difficult ones are killed— the weaklings are allowed to die of starvation—the strong ones are enslaved.

KAARLO

You are an anthropologist—a man of learning, Dr. Ziemssen. Do you approve of this technique?

ZIEMSSEN

Naturally, I regret the necessity for it. But I *admit* the necessity. And so must you, Dr. Valkonen. Remember that every great state of the past in its stages of construction has required slavery. Today, the greatest world state is in process of formation. There is a great need for slave labor. And—these Finns and Scandinavians would be useful. They are strong; they have great capacity for endurance. Is that brutal—

ruthless? Yes. But I am now talking to a scientist, not a snivelling sentimentalist. Vivisection has been called brutal, ruthless—but it is necessary for the survival of man. So it is necessary that inferior races be considered merely as animals. . . . Do you believe me, Herr Doktor?

KAARLO

I believe you. Although—still talking as one scientist to another—I cannot help wondering just how you establish proof that these other races are inferior, especially when you know it is a lie.

ZIEMSSEN

Of course it is a lie, biologically. But we can prove it by the very simple expedient of asserting our own superiority—just as the Romans did before they decayed—and the Anglo-Saxons, before *they* decayed. View this objectively, Herr Doktor, and then you will be able to proceed with your experiments. You have made important progress in an important field—conditioning men to their environment. That can be of extraordinary value to us in the future. You can help to postpone, perhaps indefinitely, the time when *we* will be conquered by decay. But, first—you must accept the theory of the new world state, for that *is* the environment of the future. If you refuse to accept, and stay here and attempt to resist destiny, you will die.

KAARLO

Where can one go to escape this world state?

ZIEMSSEN (*smiles*)

An intelligent question, Herr Doktor. I assure you that the United States is secure for the present. It may continue so for a long time, if the Americans refrain from interfering with us in Mexico and South America and Canada. And I believe they will refrain. They are now showing far greater intelligence in that respect than ever before. They are learning to mind their own shrinking business.

KAARLO

I appreciate your motives in warning me, Dr. Ziemssen. And I understand that all you have told me is confidential.

ZIEMSSEN (*laughing*)

You *are* an innocent, my friend! Nothing that I have said is confidential. You may repeat it all. And you will not be believed. There is the proof of our superiority—that our objectives are so vast that our pigmy-minded enemies simply have not the capacity to believe them. They are eager to accept the big lies we give them, because they cannot comprehend the big truth. (*Rises.*) And the big truth is this: For the first time since the whole surface of the earth became known, one dynamic race is on the march to occupy that surface and rule it! When you have absorbed that huge conception, you will find that your own theories can be adjusted to it. And now I must go. (*He extends his hand to* KAARLO.) But I advise you to make haste, Herr Doktor. Finland's only lines of communication are through Sweden and Norway. We have many means of cutting those lines. Good-bye, Herr Doktor. I said good-bye. I hope we part friends. (*He goes to the door.*)

(KAARLO *nods as he shakes hands with* DR. ZIEMSSEN.)

My compliments to Frau Valkonen. Good-bye. (*He goes.*)

UNCLE WALDEMAR'S VOICE (*heard offstage*)
Good-bye, Dr. Ziemssen.

ZIEMSSEN'S VOICE

Good-bye, Herr Sederstrum. I have so enjoyed your music.

(KAARLO *crosses and stands behind the sofa.* UNCLE WALDEMAR *enters, switches on lights, goes immediately to the windows and starts closing the black curtains.* KAARLO *looks toward the kitchen.*)

KAARLO

Uncle Waldemar—Uncle Waldemar——

UNCLE WALDEMAR

Yes. . . . What is it? (*Having fixed the windows,* UNCLE WALDEMAR *turns to* KAARLO.)

KAARLO

Get your hat and coat on.

UNCLE WALDEMAR

What for?

KAARLO

I want you to go to the American Legation and see Mr. Walsh. Tell him that Mrs. Valkonen will leave on that ship Mr. Corween told me about. I believe it sails from Goteborg on Tuesday. He must make all the necessary arrangements at once. Find out what is the earliest possible moment she can leave for Sweden. Ask him if it is safe by aeroplane.

UNCLE WALDEMAR

You're sending Miranda away—alone?

KAARLO

Yes. Be quiet. She's right there in the kitchen.

UNCLE WALDEMAR

You think you can persuade her to do this?

KAARLO

I have to persuade her, and if necessary, you will help me. You know what has happened to Poland.

UNCLE WALDEMAR

Yes, I know. But—Miranda doesn't care about those things. She doesn't believe them.

KAARLO

I didn't believe them either. . . . But—I'll find another way of persuading her. If ruthlessness is the order of this day, then I shall be ruthless, too. I will tell her I don't want her here. She is of no use in a time like this.

UNCLE WALDEMAR

That will hurt her more deeply than the Russians ever could.

KAARLO

She will recover from that hurt. Go ahead!

UNCLE WALDEMAR

Very well.

(He starts to go, but MIRANDA *enters. She is carrying a tray on which are a coffee pot and cups.)*

MIRANDA

Uncle Waldemar—I made some coffee. Would you like some?

UNCLE WALDEMAR

No, thank you.

MIRANDA

I tasted it. It's quite good.

UNCLE WALDEMAR

Thank you—but I have to go.

MIRANDA

Where?

UNCLE WALDEMAR

I want to have some exercise and fresh air.

MIRANDA

But you've been out all day.

UNCLE WALDEMAR

Even so—I'm going out again.

(*He goes out.* MIRANDA *takes the tray over to the piano and puts it down.*)

MIRANDA

Poor Uncle Waldemar—all this has upset him terribly. . . . Will you have some coffee, Kaarlo?

KAARLO

No, thank you.

MIRANDA

I wish you'd try it.

KAARLO

Later, perhaps. . . . Please sit down.

MIRANDA

What is it, Kaarlo? Do you want to talk about Erik? (*She starts to go out.*)

KAARLO

No—I do not want to talk about Erik. Please sit down.

(*She sits down and looks at him, curiously.*)
I wish to tell you, my dear, that the time has come for you to go home.

MIRANDA

Home? This is my home.

KAARLO

I mean—to your own country. To America.

MIRANDA (*amazed*)

Why?

KAARLO

Because I do not wish you to stay here. Mr. Walsh at the American Legation can make all the necessary arrangements. You will probably leave for Sweden tomorrow—perhaps even tonight. We will hear soon about that. You can then go to Boston and stay with your aunt.

MIRANDA

Will you go with me?

KAARLO

Naturally not. I am needed here. You will stay in America until this business is over.

MIRANDA

And when it *is* over? What then?

KAARLO

Why—you'll come back here, and we'll go right on living as we've always done. I might come to America and fetch you.

MIRANDA

Supposing you were killed?

KAARLO

I—killed? I'm a doctor.

MIRANDA

And do you suppose a Russian in a bombing plane ten thousand feet up can tell the difference

between an ordinary person and a winner of the
Nobel prize?

KAARLO

It is out of the question that I should go. Freud
left Vienna after the Nazi occupation. He went
to London, and he was welcomed there, he was
honored. But—he couldn't speak. He knew that if
he told the truth, it would be printed, and his own
people, still in Austria, would be made to suffer for
it, horribly. . . . So Freud was technically free—
but he was silenced. What did he then have to live
for? Nothing. . . . So he died. . . . No—I will
not leave. You must go alone.

MIRANDA

And if I left here—what would *I* have to live for?

KAARLO

Oh, you'll manage very well in your own great,
secure, distant country.

(*He has been moving about the room. Her eyes
have been following him, questioning·him, seeking
him out, with every word, every move.*)

MIRANDA

Kaarlo! Tell me the truth. Why do you want
me to go?

KAARLO

What can you do here? This is a war for the
defense of Finland. It must be fought by the Finnish people.

(*She is staring at him. He is avoiding her gaze.*)

This country becomes an armed camp. Every one of us knows what he must do, or she must do, and is trained to do it. Are you trained for anything, but wearing lovely clothes, being a charming hostess?

(*She looks at him, helplessly.*)
You are an intelligent woman, Miranda. Reason this out for yourself. You will see that this is a time when every one who eats bread must have worked to earn it. And, God help us, there is only one form of work that matters now—resistance—blind, dogged, desperate resistance.

MIRANDA (*rising, and following him*)

You've said yourself—that kind of resistance is useless.

(*She is trying desperately to score a point. He is trying desperately to avoid being scored on, though ever conscious of his vulnerability.*)

KAARLO (*angrily*)

You don't know what I've said. Or—if you know the words, you have less idea of their meaning than the youngest of the students who hear my lectures at the Institute. I'm not insulting your courage, Miranda. Nor your good will. I'm sure you would like to be useful. But you can't. You know you can't.

MIRANDA

You think it would be impossible for me to contribute anything—to help in any way?

KAARLO

Why do I have to tell you what you must know yourself?

(MIRANDA *looks at him with a look almost of bitter hostility. She turns and walks away. Unutterably miserable, he looks after her. The artifice of his frigid superiority is beginning to crumple.*) There is no reason for you to be ashamed of this. This is not your country. It is not your war.

MIRANDA

This is the country of my husband and my son.

KAARLO

And do you think Erik and I want you to be caught in these ruins?

MIRANDA

You have no right to speak of Erik! I don't think he would be particularly happy or proud to hear that his mother has scurried to safety at the first sound of a shot fired.

KAARLO

Erik has American blood in his veins. He will understand.

MIRANDA (*flaming*)

Oh! So that's it! His American blood will tell him that it's perfectly reasonable for me to run away. You evidently share Kaatri's opinion of me.

KAARLO (*desperately*)

Don't put words into my mouth that I have not uttered——

MIRANDA (*turning on him, suddenly coming to him*)

Then don't be afraid to come out and say what you mean. It's obvious that you don't want me here, because I'm incompetent—I'm a parasite—I'm a non-essential. In all these years that we've been together nothing has happened to disturb the lovely serenity of our home. And now comes this great calamity. And immediately you decide that you don't want me—you don't need me.

KAARLO

I didn't say that!

MIRANDA

Then what did you say?

(KAARLO *is obviously making a last effort to control himself.*)

KAARLO

Miranda! You don't understand why I want you to go!

MIRANDA

It makes no difference to me whether I understand it or not. There's one thing I do know, and you'd better know it, too: I am not going. Probably, you *don't* need me. You have important work to do—and I'm sure that's enough, for you. But

the time may come when Erik might need me, and
when that time comes, I intend to be here——

KAARLO

No, please—for God's sake—don't keep on bringing Erik into it! Wasn't it bad enough to see him
going away like that, in his uniform? That poor,
hopeful, defenseless child! (*He sees that he has
hurt her, terribly, with that.*) Oh—I'm sorry, darling. You must see that I've been making a desperate attempt to drive you to safety with lies.
It's no use. You always can make me tell the truth.
The real trouble is—you've had too much confidence in me. How could you know that I was living
in a dream—a beautiful, wishful dream in which
you played your own unsubstantial but exciting
part? And now—there is war—and our own son
goes to fight—and I wake up to discover that
reality itself is a hideous nightmare. . . . I
shouldn't be talking to you like this, Miranda. I'm
frightened.

MIRANDA

You can never be afraid to say anything to me,
darling.

KAARLO

I have suddenly realized what and where I am.
I am a man working in the apparent security of a
laboratory. I am working on a theory so tentative
that it may take hundreds of years of research,
and generations of workers, to prove it. I am trying to defeat insanity—degeneration of the human

race. . . . And then—a band of pyromaniacs enters the building in which I work. And that building is the world—the whole planet—not just Finland. They set fire to it. What can I do? Until that fire is put out, there can be no peace—no freedom from fear—no hope of progress for mankind. . . . Every day that we hold them off—will only serve to increase the terror of the vengeance which must surely descend upon us. All the pathetic survivors of this war will have to pay in torture for the heroism of the dead. And it isn't just us—not just this one little breed that wants to be free. This is a war for everybody—yes—even for the scientists who thought themselves immune behind their test tubes. (*He looks into her eyes again.*) Darling! I can stand this ordeal if I know it is only for myself. I can stand it if I know you are safe—that you are beyond their reach. . . . I love you. That is the only reality left to me. I love you.

(*They are in each other's arms. For a moment, they are silent.*)

Miranda

Then I can stand it, too, darling, whatever it is. I can stand it as long as I know that you love me —that you do need me—that I am essential, after all. Even if I am a woman who is nothing but a woman. Even at a time when the whole life of the world is marching with men. . . .

(*They hold each other, closely. After a moment, she rises.*)

Now come and have some coffee.

(*They cross to the piano. She feels the coffee pot.*)

It's not very warm.

KAARLO

It's no matter, darling. I'm sure it's good.

(*She is pouring the coffee.*)

CURTAIN

SCENE IV

The same. New Year's Day, 1940. Noon. There is a Christmas tree. There are many decorations on the tree, including a wide, white ribbon on which is an inscription in Finnish. At the top of the tree is a star.

UNCLE WALDEMAR *is at the piano playing something surprisingly spirited and gay.* KAARLO *comes in. He wears the uniform coat of a Colonel in the Medical Corps, but otherwise he is in civilian clothes. He is buttoning up the coat. As he glances back into the mirror, he looks rather sheepish and self-conscious.* UNCLE WALDEMAR *looks at him.*

KAARLO

Well—Uncle Waldemar—haven't you anything to say about my new uniform?

UNCLE WALDEMAR

What should I say? I've seen thousands of uniforms lately. They all look the same.

KAARLO (*laughs*)

I know. But—for some reason—when you see one on yourself, it seems to look better.

UNCLE WALDEMAR (*stops playing, rises*)

Are you trying to fool me, Kaarlo?

102

KAARLO

Fool you? Why should I——?

UNCLE WALDEMAR

You want me to think you are proud to be going?

KAARLO (*gravely*)

No, Uncle Waldemar. (*He looks off to the kitchen, and then speaks confidentially.*) When Erik went—I—I thought our world had come to an end. Since then—I have been struggling to adjust myself—to find in all this tragedy some intimation of hope for the future.

UNCLE WALDEMAR (*tenderly*)

I know, Kaarlo.

KAARLO

This (*indicates his uniform coat*) represents the final stage in that attempt at adjustment. It is like the moment when a scientist knows he can no longer experiment with guinea pigs—he must now test his theories on human life itself. It is kill or cure.

UNCLE WALDEMAR

What are those ribbons you are wearing?

KAARLO

The order of St. Ann with Swords—the Cross of St. George's.

UNCLE WALDEMAR

You're going into the Mannerheim Line wearing Russian decorations?

KAARLO

Why not? I won them. Or—at any rate—
they were given to me. You think I should leave
them off?

(MIRANDA *comes in from the kitchen with a
tray on which are a pitcher of eggnog and five
punch glasses. She sees* KAARLO's *coat.*)

MIRANDA

What is that you are wearing?

KAARLO

It is my uniform coat. I was just trying it on.

MIRANDA

What for? What do you want with a uniform?

KAARLO

Of course I should have one. I'm a Colonel in
the Army Medical Corps.

MIRANDA

Now don't tell me you want to look impressive.
Why have you suddenly got a uniform?

KAARLO

Because I have to, Miranda. I'm going to
Viipuri.

MIRANDA (*shocked*)

When are you going?

Kaarlo

This afternoon, I believe. What is that on the tray you brought in?

Miranda

It's eggnog. I promised Dave Corween I'd make some to celebrate New Year's. Why are they sending you to Viipuri?

Kaarlo

Nobody is sending me, Miranda. I'm going because I wish to. More hospital space has to be provided there, and I want to see that the work is done efficiently.

Miranda

Why haven't you told me about this before? You knew about it, Uncle Waldemar?

Uncle Waldemar

He told me only today.

Kaarlo

Now really, Miranda. This is not to be taken so seriously. I am not going very far away, and I shall probably be back within a fortnight. In fact, Dave Corween is going with me and a Polish officer named Rutkowski. Dave is to broadcast from Viipuri. That proves there's no danger. (*He starts to go out at the right.*)

Miranda

How do you get to Viipuri?

KAARLO

I go in style . . . in that new American ambulance that just arrived from France. (*He goes out taking off his coat.*)

MIRANDA (*looking after* KAARLO)

He was afraid to tell me—wasn't he, Uncle Waldemar?

UNCLE WALDEMAR

Kaarlo always likes to avoid unpleasant subjects . . . outside his laboratory.

MIRANDA

Is there something serious happening?

UNCLE WALDEMAR

Well—you know, Miranda—there is still war. They still attack.

MIRANDA

But everything's going well for us, isn't it?

UNCLE WALDEMAR

We're alive. That's more than any one expected.

MIRANDA

Why do they want more hospitals at Viipuri? I thought there weren't many wounded.

UNCLE WALDEMAR

That is because now most of the wounded are frozen to death before they can be brought in. When warmer weather comes—the fighting will be different. They will need hospitals—especially on the isthmus.

(*She considers this dreadful thought for a moment.*)

MIRANDA (*desperately*)

Oh, God—Uncle Waldemar. Why don't we hear from Erik? He has been gone a whole month— *why* don't we hear?

(UNCLE WALDEMAR *comes to her.*)

UNCLE WALDEMAR

We know Erik is well. Kaarlo sees every casualty list—including even those who are sick. It's just that up there in the Arctic there is not much chance of sending letters.

(*The doorbell is heard.*)

MIRANDA

There's the doorbell.

UNCLE WALDEMAR

I'll go, Miranda. (UNCLE WALDEMAR *goes out.*)

(VOICES *can be heard off at the right*)
How do you do, Mr. Corween?

DAVE (*off*)

How do you do, sir?

UNCLE WALDEMAR (*off*)
Happy New Year!

DAVE (*off*)

Happy New Year to you, sir!

UNCLE WALDEMAR (*off*)

Go right in.

DAVE (*off*)

Thank you. (DAVE *comes in. He is dressed for a cold journey.*)

MIRANDA

Dave! Happy New Year!

DAVE

Happy New Year, Mrs. Valkonen.

MIRANDA (*pointing to the tray*)

I've kept my promise about the eggnog.

DAVE

I'm afraid I'm going to overtax your hospitality. There are four other boys here, all going up with the ambulance.

MIRANDA

Oh! Bring them all in.

DAVE

Thank you. (*He calls off.*) Come in, boys. Come in, Major.

(MAJOR RUTKOWSKI *comes in. He is a tired, tragic young Polish officer. He is followed almost at once by* JOE BURNETT, BEN GICHNER *and* FRANK OLMSTEAD. JOE *is tall, lean, wearing a smart, new aviator's uniform;* BEN *is stout and cheerful;* FRANK, *young, sensitive and serious-minded. Both* BEN *and* FRANK *wear uniforms of the American Ambulance Corps, with Red Cross insignia on the sleeves.*)

DAVE

Mrs. Valkonen—this is Major Rutkowski.

RUTKOWSKI (*bows*)

Madame.

MIRANDA

How do you do?

DAVE

And this is the American Expeditionary Force in Finland. Joe Burnett of Haverford, Pa.——

MIRANDA (*shaking hands with each in turn*)

How do you do?

DAVE

Ben Gichner of Cincinnati.

MIRANDA

I'm very glad to see you.

DAVE

And Frank Olmstead of San Francisco. Mrs. Valkonen of New Bedford.

MIRANDA

Happy New Year!

JOE

Thank you, Mrs. Valkonen.

FRANK

Thank you.

BEN

And a very happy New Year to you, Madame.

MIRANDA

I have some eggnog, gentlemen——
(*Their faces light up.*)

In the midst of war we still have some milk and eggs and rye whiskey and even a little cream. You start serving it, Dave—while I get some more glasses. Sit down, everybody. (*She goes out through the dining room.*)

DAVE (*crossing*)

Come on, Joe.

(JOE *and* FRANK *follow* DAVE *across.* BEN *and* RUTKOWSKI *are looking about the room.*)

Now, boys, remember. No remarks about the horrors of war. I'm afraid Mrs. Valkonen feels pretty badly about her husband going.

JOE

We'll be tactful, Dave.

RUTKOWSKI (*quietly*)

A lovely house. This would be the house of good people in any country.

BEN

It's got a sort of nice, Victorian quality. I thought everything in Finland was moderne.

FRANK (*who is looking at the photographs on the piano*)

Look, Joe. . . . Doctor Jung, Alexis Carrel, President Masaryk——

DAVE (*bringing drinks across to* RUTKOWSKI *and* BEN)

Here you are, Major Rutkowski. Nourishing and stimulating—but apt to be dangerous.

(FRANK *is standing by the piano, playing a few bars of a swing tune.*)

MIRANDA (*offstage*)

Have you tried it yet?

DAVE

We were waiting for you, Mrs. Valkonen.

(MIRANDA *re-enters with a tray holding more glasses.* BEN *and* RUTKOWSKI *rise.* DAVE *takes the tray from her, goes to the serving table and pours drinks for* MIRANDA *and himself.*)

MIRANDA

Here you are—here are the glasses. (*To* FRANK.) Was that you playing?

FRANK (*diffidently*)

I wouldn't call it playing.

MIRANDA

It is wonderful.

BEN

Come on, Dave. I think you ought to make a little speech in behalf of all of us.

Dave

I'm not at my best without a mike and a coast-to-coast hook-up. (*He raises his glass and addresses* Miranda.) However, we want to tell you we're glad to be here, enjoying your gracious hospitality, and we hope that this New Year will bring you and yours health and happiness.

Miranda (*as the circle of men gathers about her*)

Why, that was a charming speech, Dave. I wish the same to you, all of you, and I welcome you to this house and this country. And I'd like to sing the Polish national anthem and "The Star-Spangled Banner," but I don't know the words of either.

Dave (*laughs*)

That's all right, Mrs. Valkonen. Neither do we. (*They all drink.*)

Joe

It's magnificent.

Dave

Mrs. Valkonen, it's better even than the Parker House Punch.

Ben

Frankly, I love it.

Frank

So do I.

Rutkowski

I've never tasted anything quite like it before—but I'm glad to be introduced.

MIRANDA

Thank you—thank you. (*To* FRANK.) Do go on playing. Help yourselves as long as it lasts. There are American cigarettes.

(MIRANDA *sits on the sofa.* FRANK *goes to the piano and plays.*)

DAVE

Everybody admires your house, Mrs. Valkonen.

BEN

Yes. I was just saying, it has a nice, old-fashioned quality.

RUTKOWSKI

It is so graceful.

MIRANDA

I'm glad you see it with the Christmas tree. That always makes it more cheerful.

FRANK (*stops playing*)

May I ask—what is the inscription on that ribbon?

MIRANDA

It's Finnish for "Glory to God in the highest and, on earth, peace, good will to men." (*A pause.*) We have that on the tree every Christmas. It's a tradition in this country.

KAARLO (*calling from off stage, at the right*)

I'll be with you in a moment, gentlemen. I have to assemble my kit.

MIRANDA (*calling to him*)

Can I help you, Kaarlo?

KAARLO (*off*)

No, thank you, my dear. Is the eggnog good, gentlemen?

DAVE

It's superb!

BEN

We're in no hurry to leave, Doctor. We're having a fine time.

MIRANDA

Have all you gentlemen just arrived in Helsinki?

BEN

We got here yesterday, ma'am. . . . I mean, Frank Olmstead and Joe Burnett and me. We came by ship from Paris to Norway. Major Rutkowski has been here since November.

MIRANDA

Had you been in the war in Poland, Major?

RUTKOWSKI

Yes, Madame, but it lasted only three weeks. I was in the cavalry.

MIRANDA

How did you manage to get here?

RUTKOWSKI

From Riga, Madame. The survivors of my regiment were driven over the Lithuanian border. I worked my way to Helsinki intending to go on through Sweden to France to join the Polish Legion there. But——

MIRANDA

But—there was a war here, so you didn't have to look any further.

RUTKOWSKI

Yes, Madame.

MIRANDA

We used to listen to Dave when he was broadcasting from Warsaw, describing the incredible heroism during the siege. Day after day we'd hear the German official radio announcing that Warsaw had fallen and then, late at night, we'd hear the government's station, playing Chopin's "Polonaise," to let us know they were still there.

BEN

We heard it, too, in Paris. It was thrilling.

DAVE

What were you doing in Paris, Ben—if it isn't too personal a question?

BEN

I was employed there! I worked for the American Express Company. I was a travel salesman. (*He turns to* MIRANDA.) I've sold many tours to picturesque Scandinavia and the Baltic, but this is my first visit to these parts.

MIRANDA

We're very glad that you're here.

BEN

Thank you.

MIRANDA

And what were you doing, Mr. Burnett?

JOE

For the last two years I've been in jail—in one of General Franco's mediæval dungeons.

MIRANDA

You fought in Spain?

JOE

Yes, Mrs. Valkonen.

MIRANDA

Why, you're a hero, Mr. Burnett.

JOE

No, Mrs. Valkonen. No hero. Just a bum. I went to Spain only because I was kicked out of Princeton.

DAVE

What for?

JOE

For throwing forward passes in chapel.

BEN

All fliers are a little crazy. Now, you take Frank and me—we're sane. We're ambulance drivers.

We're non-combatants, we hope. We'll have a good safe view of this country. And what I want to see most is some of those ski troops.

(DAVE *looks at him, sharply.*)

Will there be any of them around Viipuri?

JOE

They're all up in the north, aren't they?

MIRANDA

Yes. They're in the north. (*Noticing* JOE's *empty glass.*) Let me get you some more. (*She takes* JOE's *glass, rises and crosses to the serving table.*)

DAVE (*rising*)

You won't see much action around Viipuri. The Mannerheim Line is just about as quiet as the Western Front.

MIRANDA

Dave is always reassuring—at least when he's talking to me. But I think he's less optimistic when he's broadcasting the news.

DAVE

That's only because I have to dramatize things for the radio audience. They like to be scared. In fact, every night, when I'm on the air, I have to remember that I'm in competition with a thriller program called "Renfrew of the Mounted."

FRANK

I used to listen to that program. Renfrew always gets his man.

(MIRANDA *looks at* FRANK, *surprised at his first contribution to the conversation.*)

MIRANDA

Did Dave say you lived in San Francisco?

FRANK

Yes, Mrs. Valkonen.

MIRANDA

And how long have you been away from home?

FRANK

I came abroad just last summer. I was going to the Sorbonne in Paris.

MIRANDA

Oh! You're a student.

FRANK

Yes, I am. I had an exchange scholarship from my own school, Leland Stanford.

MIRANDA

You must be brilliant! What sort of things were you studying?

FRANK

Well—I particularly wanted to study French verse forms. I realize it sounds pretty ridiculous——

BEN

The terrible truth is that Frank wants to be a poet. (BEN *has to laugh at that.*)

MIRANDA

Now, really—I don't see anything to laugh at.

FRANK

Perhaps you would if you could read any of my attempts.

MIRANDA

I'd love to read some of your poetry. When I was a young girl, my greatest hero was Rupert Brooke. Maybe now that you're here—and have all this experience—maybe you'll write as he did. "Honour has come back, as a king to earth, And paid his subjects with a royal wage; and Nobleness walks in our ways again; and we have come into our heritage."

FRANK

I'm afraid I could never write like Rupert Brooke, even if I were that good. He was always singing of the heroism of war.

MIRANDA

Oh! And you see it as unheroic?

FRANK

Yes, Mrs. Valkonen. I do.

BEN

In addition to being a poet—Frank is also a rabid pacifist.

MIRANDA

I'm glad to hear it. My husband is a pacifist,

too. You must have a talk with him while you're driving to Viipuri.

FRANK

I hope I have that privilege.

BEN

I've been a pacifist myself, in my time. I used to think, I'll never let my children grow up to get into this mass murder. But now I've got to the stage of figuring I ought to help put the murderers out of business *before* my children grow up and have to fight 'em themselves.

DAVE

Have you got any children, Ben?

BEN

No. It was all hypothetical.

MIRANDA

But you came here, to Finland. You came through mine fields and submarines, didn't you?

FRANK

Yes, we did.

MIRANDA

What made you come through all that into this little war?

FRANK

Because I'm a crazy fool, that's why.

Miranda

That's interesting. How many crazy fools do you suppose there are in America?

Dave

I can name four hundred and seventy-three of my own acquaintance.

Ben

The pioneers were fools. And as for that goof Columbus—why didn't *he* stay home and mind his own business? (*He is crossing to help himself to another glass of eggnog.*)

Dave

Go easy on that punch, Ben. You've got to drive the ambulance.

Ben

You can count on me, Dave.

Miranda (*to* Rutkowski)

Have you ever met any Americans before, Major?

Rutkowski

No, I'm sorry, I have not.

Miranda

Then this will give you a faint idea.

Rutkowski

I am glad of the opportunity. I have often won-

dered what it could be like to be an American—
to believe, even for a moment, that such things as
peace and security are possible. You see, we have
never been permitted such belief. For us, the sun
rose each morning among our enemies—and it set
among our enemies. And now, it is high noon,
and our enemies have joined together over our
country—and we are gone.

DAVE

It isn't always so completely delightful to be an
American, Major. Sometimes even we have an
uncomfortable feeling of insecurity. I imagine
that Pontius Pilate didn't feel entirely at peace
with himself. He knew that this was a good, just
man, who didn't deserve death. He was against a
crown of thorns on principle. But when they
cried, "Crucify Him!" all Pilate could say was,
"Bring me a basin of water, so that I can wash
my hands of the whole matter."

(KAARLO *comes in, dressed in his uniform.*
UNCLE WALDEMAR *comes after him. All the guests
rise.*)

KAARLO

No—please—don't get up. Gentlemen—this is
my Uncle, Mr. Sederstrum.

UNCLE WALDEMAR

How do you do?

(*All greet him.* MIRANDA *is staring at* KAARLO
in his uniform. He looks at her, smiles lamely.)

KAARLO

Now I'll have a glass of that eggnog. Then I suppose we should go?

RUTKOWSKI (*looking at his watch*)

I'm afraid so.

MIRANDA

Bring a glass for Uncle Waldemar too, Dave.

BEN

To think that I should be going to Viipuri in company with a winner of the Nobel Prize.

KAARLO

I hope we don't get lost on the way. I have no sense of direction whatever. We'll rely on Major Rutkowski to guide us. The Major has been in the Mannerheim Line. Did he tell you about it?

(*This to* MIRANDA, *as she pours his eggnog.*)

MIRANDA

No. He didn't.

KAARLO

Oh—he says it's very dull there. (*He lifts his glass.*) Well, gentlemen, I beg leave to drink to you, our friends from the United States and from Poland.

(*They all move into a circle at the left.*)

DAVE

Thank you, Doctor.

RUTKOWSKI

And long life to the Republic of Finland!

ALL

Hear, hear!

BEN

And to you, Doctor.
(*They drink.*)

KAARLO

Why, Miranda, it's good! Why don't we have this every day?

(FRANK *goes to the piano and starts playing "Auld Lang Syne." All sing. . . . KAATRI comes in at the right. She wears the Lotta uniform. She is very pale.*)

MIRANDA

Kaatri! (*She goes quickly to KAATRI, who is looking wildly around the room at all the strangers.*)

KAATRI

Mrs. Valkonen—I had to see you——

MIRANDA

Have you heard from Erik?

KAATRI

No. But I must talk to you——

DAVE

Come on, boys. Get your coats and hats on. We'll wait outside, Mrs. Valkonen.

JOE

Certainly.
(*They start to go out.*)

MIRANDA

You'll forgive me, Major Rutkowski. We'll be out in just a moment.

RUTKOWSKI

Of course.
(RUTKOWSKI *goes out at the right after* DAVE, JOE, BEN *and* FRANK.)

MIRANDA

Now, Kaatri dear—what is it?

KAATRI

I've written every day to Erik. I haven't heard from him since that first letter two weeks ago. I've got to see him, Mrs. Valkonen. Don't you think they could give him a little leave?

MIRANDA

He'll surely have leave soon, dear. The Russians have to stop attacking some time. Isn't that so, Kaarlo?

KAARLO

Of course it is. Erik's all right. In fact, he's probably enjoying himself. He likes that energetic life. Now—really—I must go. . . . (*He starts to say good-bye to* UNCLE WALDEMAR.)

KAATRI

No—please, Dr. Valkonen. There's something I have to ask you. I'm going to have a baby.

MIRANDA (*rising*)

Darling. (*She takes her in her arms.*)

KAARLO

Well! I'm very happy to hear it.

KAATRI

I'm not happy. I don't want it! Dr. Valkonen! What can I do to stop it? Please tell me what I can do.

MIRANDA

You're not ashamed, Kaatri? There's nothing for you to be ashamed of.

KAATRI

No—I'm not! But I don't want it. You've got to help me, Dr. Valkonen.

KAARLO

Have you told your family of this?

KAATRI

No. It wouldn't be easy for them to understand, as you do, about Erik and me.

MIRANDA

Why don't you want to have a baby, Kaatri?

KAATRI

I'm working. It would make me useless—just another person to be cared for——

Miranda

That's not being useless.

Kaatri

It is now! What good would it be to bring a child into a world like this? He would have no country—no hope. *Please*, Dr. Valkonen. I'm sorry to be troubling you. But—just tell me some doctor that I can see.

Kaarlo

You will see Dr. Palm. Miranda—you know him.

Miranda

Yes, Kaarlo.

Kaarlo

You take Kaatri to see him. Tell him that this is our daughter-in-law, and her baby will be our grandchild.

(Kaatri *looks at him, with terror.*)

Yes, my dear, you are going to have that child.

Kaatri (*hysterical*)

No—no! I won't have it! (*She tries desperately to break away from them.*) I won't have a child born under a curse!

Miranda

Quiet, dear. Please. (*She seats* Kaatri *beside her.*)

Kaatri (*making another frantic attempt to get away*)

No! You won't help me. I'll find a doctor——

Kaarlo

Do as my wife tells you, Kaatri! You love Erik,
and he loves you. You were willing to be married
to him. You have taken responsibility. The highest responsibility! You are not going to evade it.

Miranda

Kaatri—Kaatri!
(*Kaatri submits. Kaarlo leans over her.*)

Kaarlo

Whatever happens to our country, your child
will not be born under a curse. It will be born to
the greatest opportunity that any child has ever
known, since the beginning of time. Remember
that, and be brave. . . . Now—I can't keep them
waiting. Good-bye, Uncle Waldemar. I'll be back
soon.

Uncle Waldemar

Yes, Kaarlo. Good-bye.
(*They kiss. Kaarlo leans over and kisses
Kaatri's head. Then he takes Miranda's hand.
She rises, looks back, motions to Uncle Walde-
mar to come to Kaatri.*)

Kaarlo

Come on, darling.
(*They go out at the right. Kaatri is crumpled
up on the couch. Uncle Waldemar goes over to
her, sits down beside her, and takes her in his
arms.*)

Uncle Waldemar

Now—don't cry, Kaatri. Pay attention to what Dr. Valkonen told you. *He* knows what he is saying. If he tells you there is good hope, you can believe him.

Curtain

SCENE V

Dave Corween's room in the Hotel Kamp in Helsinki.

It is evening.

Upper right is a door leading to the corridor. At the left is a door leading to a bedroom.

The room is in pretty much of a mess. At the right, on a chair, is DAVE's *typewriter, with copy paper and carbon strewn about. At the left, is a large table, on which is the same broadcasting apparatus seen in the first scene.*

DAVE *is at the microphone reading from a typescript before him.* GUS *is up-stage, left, with his earphones on.*

DAVE

In an attempt to surround the main force of the Finnish army on the Karelian Isthmus, the Russians are now making determined attacks across Viipuri Bay. The Mannerheim Line, supposedly impregnable bulwark of Finland's defense, has been shattered. The bombardment of these defenses, and of Viipuri itself, has now reached the terrible total of three hundred thousand shells a day. Looking at the ruination in Viipuri, I could not help thinking of the despairing prophecies made by H. G. Wells in *The Shape of Things to Come.* Here was the awful picture of the collapse of our Western civilization, the beginning of the Age of Frustration. Stores and factories, public libraries, museums, movie theatres—hospitals and schools and homes—all reduced to junk heaps. The Soviet Union is being generous in the expenditure of its ammunition, and extravagantly generous with the life blood of its men. Never again will these workers of the world arise! But in Moscow, the official propaganda bureau broadcasts constantly in Finnish, sending soothing encouragement to this beleaguered little country. Today I heard them say, and I quote, "The Red Army sends greetings to the workers of Finland. The Red Army does not destroy. That is why the workers in every country love the Red Army." And—perhaps, in the end—"love" will conquer all. . . . This is David Corween in Helsinki, returning you now to C. B. S. in New York.

(Gus *switches off the radio.* Dave *turns to* Joe.) How was that, Joe? Do you think I'm holding my own against Renfrew of the Mounted?

Joe

I think you're wasting your breath, Dave. Nobody's listening.

Gus

I don't see how they can—with the complicated hook-up we've got now. And if one of those bombs today had landed fifty yards farther west, there wouldn't be any broadcasting station here at all. Did you see those craters?

DAVE

Yes.

GUS

Boy! They must be dropping those two-ton bombs now, like they had in Spain.

DAVE

Are you going to be flying around here now to protect us, Joe?

JOE

I doubt it. I guess I'll get shipped right back to the lines.

GUS

Well, I hope they don't keep us here until it's too late to get out. I'd hate to go through Warsaw again. I think I'll go down and see if I can get a cup of coffee. Where's the sugar?

DAVE

Here. (*He hands* GUS *an envelope filled with sugar that has been lying on the couch.*)

GUS (*to* JOE)

See you later.

JOE

Sure.

(GUS *goes out.*)

Say, Dave—when you were in Viipuri, did you see anything of Ben and Frank and Dr. Valkonen?

DAVE

Yes. They got their hospitals established there and now they're working day and night to evacuate

them. Ben and Frank don't seem to be having a
very good time in this war.

JOE

I guess they're in a tough spot now, with those
attacks across Viipuri Bay.

DAVE

Yes, I've got to go and see Mrs. Valkonen and
try to think of something encouraging to say.
Last week I was up in the north. I saw some of the
ski troops in action.

JOE

Did you see Mrs. Valkonen's son?

DAVE

No. But I got an idea of what he must be going
through. Poor kid. I remember the first time I
came here he said that Finland wouldn't. be in
danger unless there was a counter-revolution in
Russia. He had that much faith in them. Well—it
seems that the counter-revolution has come.

JOE

Something else has come. I saw something today that might interest you.

DAVE

What was it?

JOE

Maybe I oughtn't to be talking to the press.

DAVE

Now listen, Joe—have another drink.

Joe

Thanks. (*He pours himself another drink.*)

Dave

You understand, Joe. Anything you tell me will be considered strictly confidential. I'll only try to pass it on the A.P., the U.P. and the radio audience. But the censorship will stop me, so your secrets will be sacred.

(Joe *drinks.*)

Joe

Well, they sent me·out reconnoitering. I wanted to know what was the greatest point of Russian concentration. I had to fly very low. The weather was closing in and the ceiling was only seven or eight hundred feet, when I was coming back. I couldn't find the field I took off from. That's why I had to fly back here to make my report to the war office.

Dave

What did you report, Joe?

Joe

I saw some staff cars coming up to the town that seemed to be general headquarters. I didn't know the name of the town, but I identified it for them on the map. I dived to give those cars a few bursts. They were full of staff officers, all right. But they weren't Russians. They were Nazis. It gave me a thrill. All this time, in fighting the Russians, I've felt just a little bit uncomfortable—you can imagine it, Dave, after my experience with the Loyalists. You know, I couldn't help saying, "God forgive them—for they know not what they do." If that's the right quotation.

DAVE

It's good enough.

JOE

But when I saw those Nazis—those arrogant bastards—and I could even see the looks on their faces—all I could think of was, "God forgive *me* if I miss this glorious opportunity." I let 'em have it. It was a beautiful sight to see 'em diving into the ditches, mussing their slick gray uniforms in the mud.

DAVE

Did you get any of them?

JOE

I'm afraid I'll never know. It was just then that the Russian planes came up. And I had to take my ship away from there.

DAVE

I thought it was about time for the Nazis to be taking a hand in this war. No wonder the tide of battle has turned. I guess they've decided there has been enough of this nonsense of Finland's resistance. Probably they want the Russians to get busy somewhere else.

(JOE *puts his glass down and stands up.*)

JOE

Is there any news from home?

DAVE

Yes. . . . This has been the biggest season in the history of Miami Beach. The University of Southern California won the national basketball championship. The Beaux Arts Ball was an outstanding success.

(JOE *crosses and looks into the bedroom at the left.*)

JOE

Good! Say, Dave—can I have the use of that elegant bathtub of yours?

DAVE

Certainly. There may be some hot water, and maybe not.

JOE

How are you fixed for a clean shirt and underwear and socks? (JOE *goes into the bedroom.*)

DAVE

I guess Gus and I can fit you out between us.

(DAVE *follows* JOE *out. There is a knock at the door at the right.*)

Come in!

(MIRANDA *comes in. Her face is pale. She comes in quietly, closing the door behind her.* DAVE *calls from off left.*)

I'll be right out.

(MIRANDA *looks around the room, then sits*

down. After a moment DAVE *comes back, and is startled to see her.*)

Mrs. Valkonen! (*He closes the bedroom door behind him.*)

MIRANDA

Hello, Dave. I hope I'm not disturbing you. Mr. Shuman told me I might come up—I met him in the lobby.

DAVE

Of course, Mrs. Valkonen. I apologize for the mess here. . . . Would you like anything to drink?

MIRANDA

No, thank you. I came to ask you for some help, Dave.

DAVE

Anything that I can do——

MIRANDA

I want to get my daughter-in-law out of this country.

DAVE

Your daughter-in-law? (*He sits down, near her.*)

MIRANDA

Yes. You've met her—Kaatri. She was married a few days ago to my son, Erik. They were married in the hospital, before he died.

DAVE

Oh—I'm terribly sorry.

Miranda

I know you're sorry, Dave. . . . Kaatri is going to have a baby. . . . She's very ill. I've made all the arrangements to get her to Norway, and then to New York. But she has to leave right away. I need some American money, Dave. Could you lend me fifty dollars? It will be paid back.

Dave

Will that be enough?

Miranda

Oh, yes—that will be plenty. And— (*She opens her handbag and takes out a sheet of paper.*) — here is the name and address of my aunt in Boston. When you get back to America, just write to her and tell her where to send the money.

(*Dave takes the paper and puts it down on the table. He takes out his wallet.*)
You see—the Finnish money is worth very little in foreign exchange now. By the time Kaatri arrives in New York, it might be completely worthless. That's why I had to have dollars. If it's inconvenient for you—I'm sure I can get it somewhere else—so please don't hesitate to——

Dave

It's perfectly convenient, and I'm very much flattered that you came to me. (*He gives her the fifty dollars.*)

Miranda

Thank you. We had an awful time persuading Kaatri to go. We never could have persuaded her if she weren't too ill to resist. She's strong—but there are limits. (*She puts the money in her handbag.*)

Dave

I wish you were going with her.

Miranda

I wish I could. I should like to be present at the birth of my grandchild. Poor Kaatri. She'll have a bad time of it, all alone there. . . . Perhaps she'll have a son, and he'll grow up a nice, respectable New Englander and go to Harvard and wonder why he has an odd name like Valkonen. . . . Erik wasn't very badly wounded. He might have pulled through if he hadn't been in such a state of terrible exhaustion. It was a lucky thing that we learned where he was and got to him. I sent word to Kaarlo. I don't know where he is—somewhere around Viipuri. (*She looks at* Dave.) They're getting closer, aren't they, Dave?

Dave

Yes.

(Miranda *rises.*)

Miranda

I'm very grateful for that loan. I hope you will come to see Uncle Waldemar and me. We're always there.

DAVE

Thank you, Mrs. Valkonen. I—I wish to God you'd let me really *do* something.

MIRANDA

But you've done a lot, Dave. That fifty dollars——

DAVE

It's not much satisfaction to know that fifty dollars is the best I can do.

MIRANDA

It's all I want, Dave. All I can use. I was desperately anxious to get Kaatri out of the country. You can understand why. It means one little link with the future. It gives us the illusion of survival—and perhaps it isn't just an illusion. . . . Good-bye, Dave.

DAVE

Good-bye.

(MIRANDA *goes out.*)

CURTAIN

SCENE VI

Classroom in a little country schoolhouse in eastern Finland. It is afternoon of a gloomy day, a few days after the preceding scene.

This schoolhouse is new and clean, designed in the most modern style. Huge, opaque glass windows would admit plenty of soft sunshine if there were any today.

At the center upstage is a dais. Before it is a row of pupil's desks. The size of these desks indicates that this is a classroom for little children of nine or ten. There is a blackboard with arithmetical problems. On the walls are tacked rows of sketches done by the pupils. Around the room on the walls are painted, in decorative, colored Finnish script, the first ten lines of the "Kalevala." (Of course, half of these lines are on the walls which we do not see.) On the window sills, little plants are sprouting in pots.

There is a door at the extreme left, leading to the little enclosed porch, and a door at the extreme right, leading to another schoolroom.

At one of the pupils' desks, the right one, GOS-DEN is sitting solemnly playing solitaire with an old, dirty pack. He is a mild, tired Englishman, about forty years old. He wears the uniform of an infantry soldier. His rifle lies on the desk be-

141

*fore him. There is a scuffle at the door, left.
GOSDEN leaps to his feet, picks up his rifle and
aims it at the door. BEN GICHNER and FRANK
OLMSTEAD come in. Both carry large haversacks.
Both are very cold.*

GOSDEN

Who are you?
(BEN *and* FRANK *raise their arms immediately.*)

BEN

Friends! We're not Russians and we're not
armed.

GOSDEN (*lowering his rifle*)

Glad to see you. Sorry but I'm a bit jumpy
these days.

BEN

That's all right, pal.

GOSDEN

Americans, eh!

BEN

That's right. What are you—English?

GOSDEN

Yes. The name is Gosden. I don't rightly know
what my rank is in this army, but I call myself
"Sergeant."

BEN (*crossing and shaking hands with* GOSDEN)

Glad to know you, Sergeant. My name is Ben
Gichner—this is Frank Olmstead.

FRANK

Glad to know you. (FRANK *sits at the desk at the left.*)

GOSDEN

Thank you. It's a pleasure to have your company. I was getting the wind up, all alone here. (*Sees their uniforms.*) You chaps in the Medical Corps?

BEN

Yes. Ambulance drivers. Only—we've lost our ambulance—it's frozen stiff as a goat in a snowdrift. When the Russians occupy this territory they'll come into possession of a Buick.

GOSDEN

You wouldn't have much use for it here. There haven't been many wounded since we retreated from the Mannerheim Line. Only dead and missing.

(FRANK *rests his head on his arms.*)

FRANK

How far are the Russians from here?

GOSDEN

I wish I knew. They've probably occupied those islands out there in Viipuri Bay. Maybe they've already reached this shore. All I can say is the last time I saw them they were coming in this direction, driving us across the ice. I've been retreating across the ice for days. I've felt like a bloody Eskimo. (*He looks about the room.*) Nice little schoolhouse, this. (*He reaches in his pocket.*) Like a bit of chocolate?

FRANK

No, thanks.

BEN (*sitting up*)

I'll have some.

GOSDEN (*tossing him some candy*)

It's good for energy.

BEN

Thanks, pal.

FRANK

How long have you been in this war?

GOSDEN

I joined up in London, just after Christmas.

FRANK

Why? What did you want to come here for?

GOSDEN (*smiles*)

Are you trying to trap me into making any remarks about fighting for freedom and democracy?

FRANK (*wearily*)

No.

GOSDEN

Because I had enough of *that* muck when I fought in the last war!

FRANK

I'm just interested to know why *any*body volunteered.

GOSDEN

Well, you might say that my case is no different from any of the others. I came because I was bored, fed up. My wife and two little children were sent to Cornwall in the evacuation. Then I lost my job. I was working in the furniture department at Harrod's—and who wants to buy furniture in war time? I couldn't join up with our own army—too old. All I could do was walk the streets looking at nothing. There was no news to read in the papers except about heroic little Finland. On Christmas, I felt I couldn't stick it out any longer. So—I thought—why not have a go at heroic little Finland? And here I am. Where I shall be tomorrow, I really couldn't say.

(RUTKOWSKI *comes in from the left, followed by* KAARLO, *who wears a Red Cross arm band on his uniform. All the men rise to attention.*)

RUTKOWSKI

At ease! Are there any more men here?

GOSDEN

No, sir. Only me. I was with Captain Vertti's company, but we got separated. I didn't know just where to go next, sir, so I stopped here for a bit of a rest.

RUTKOWSKI

Has there been much shelling here?

GOSDEN

I've heard plenty of heavies, overhead, but none dropping here, sir. There's also been a lot of Bolshie planes, flying low—looking the situation over, I expect.

RUTKOWSKI

They're probably shelling the railroad line between Viipuri and Helsinki. Trying to cut off all possibilities of re-enforcement. I'm going out to find if there is any one in command here.

(KAARLO *is greatly interested in the schoolroom. He crosses to the right.*)

KAARLO

This schoolhouse would do well for a field ambulance station.

(BEN *and* FRANK *have sat down.*)

GOSDEN (*still standing*)

Begging your pardon, sir. You couldn't find a more exposed place.

RUTKOWSKI

Yes—you might say that this *is* Finland—small —clean—and exposed. (*With a slight shrug.*) I shall be back presently, Doctor. (*He goes out at the left.*)

KAARLO

We'll be waiting, Major. (*To* GOSDEN.) I'm Dr. Valkonen. How do you do?

(*Somewhat to* GOSDEN's *surprise,* KAARLO *extends his hand. They shake.*)

GOSDEN

Thank you, sir. My name is Gosden.

KAARLO

I gather that things here are a bit disorganized.

GOSDEN

And no wonder, sir. It's a miracle that there's any sign of an army left—the way they've been pushing us.

(GOSDEN *sits.* KAARLO *crosses to the dais and looks at the blackboard.*)

KAARLO

You know—they must have left this school very quickly—right in the midst of an arithmetic lesson. Look—there's a multiplication problem that was never finished. The pupils were probably delighted but— (*pointing to the sketches*) —they evidently had to leave without knowing which picture won first prize.

BEN

How old would the kids be in a school like this?

KAARLO

From seven to twelve I should judge. It's just a little country school. I wish you could see it when the children are here. The boys are on that side, the girls there. When the teacher comes in, the boys all rise and bow stiffly. The girls make their little curtsys. Maybe in their hearts they loathe the teacher—but they're always very polite. And all very full of moral preachments. Oh, yes. . . . You see that inscription all around the walls? That's from the Kalevala—the epic poem of Finland. It had its beginnings in the songs of our minstrels a thousand years ago. Your poet, Longfellow, knew the Kalevala and used its rhythm in Hiawatha. (*He looks up, and starts to recite, at first with a sort of tender amusement, and then with increasing solemnity. His eyes travel about the room as he follows the inscription.*)

"Let us clasp our hands together,
  Let us interlock our fingers;
  Let us sing a cheerful measure,
  Let us use our best endeavors
  While our dear ones hearken to us,
  And our loved ones are instructed,
  While the young are standing round us,
  Of the rising generation,
  Let them learn the words of magic,
  And recall our songs and legends."

(*He is quiet for a moment, looking toward the right. Then he turns to the others.*)

Every Finnish child learns about the Kalevala—just as Americans learn those words about Life, Liberty and the Pursuit of Happiness.

FRANK (*earnestly*)

Dr. Valkonen——

KAARLO

Yes, Frank?

FRANK

I've wanted to ask you a question——

KAARLO

Yes?

FRANK

About your book— (FRANK *pulls a paper-cov-
ered book, badly dog-eared, from his jacket
pocket.*)

KAARLO

You've been carrying that around with you?

FRANK

Yes. I bought it in Viipuri when we first went
there.

BEN

Frank is more worried about your book, Doctor,
than he is about the Russians.

FRANK (*he opens the book to the last page*)

There's a lot of it I don't understand, but what
I wanted to ask you about most is the very end.

KAARLO

What is it at the end?

FRANK (*reads*)

"How long, O Lord, before we shall hear the
sound of the Seventh Angel of the Apocalypse?
Have you forgotten the promise of St. John? 'And

they shall see his face, and his name shall be in their foreheads. And there shall be no night there and they need no candle, neither light of the sun; for the Lord giveth them light; and they shall reign forever and ever.' How long, O Lord, before we shall be given to see the true revelation?" (FRANK *closes the book and looks at* KAARLO.) Why did you conclude a scientific work with Biblical words—and what do you mean by the true revelation?

KAARLO (*simply*)

It's the revealing to us of ourselves—of what we are—and what we may be. (*Smiles.*) Of course— we can all use the Book of Revelation to substantiate our own theories. It's an eternally effective device. I have heard evangelist charlatans quote it to prove that if you do not accept their nonsense and pay for it, you will most surely burn in hell. But there is something profound in those words I quoted. That unknown Jewish mystic who wrote that—somehow, unconsciously, he knew that man will find the true name of God in his own forehead, in the mysteries of his own mind. "And there shall be no night there." That is the basis of all the work I have done.

FRANK

And how do you feel about that work now, Dr. Valkonen?

KAARLO

I think I've learned a great deal in the last few months. Research work in the field! I never dreamed I would have such a vast laboratory, with so many specimens.

BEN

Have you arrived at any new conclusions, Doctor?

KAARLO

Not conclusions, I'm afraid. Just—somewhat stronger suspicions. It is wonderful to see what men are capable of—what courage—what endurance—what utter lack of selfishness. And what a tragedy that these heroic qualities can be tested only by disease. That's what all this is, you know —disease. All of this—reasonless war—aimless revolution—it's a psychological epidemic. (*He rises. It is as though he were lecturing to a class.*) Scientists had seen it coming, for a long time, long before 1914, even. But we had no conception of its extent. And now the very belief of men that they can insulate themselves against it is in itself a sign of lunacy. The germs of that disease travel on the air waves. The only defenses are still here— behind the forehead. . . . (*He pauses and smiles, looking particularly at* GOSDEN.) I apologize, gentlemen, for carrying on a conversation which must be extremely boring to you.

GOSDEN

I'm an ignorant man, sir. I haven't read this book. I didn't even know I was in the presence of any one who had written a book. But—from what you've said—I have a feeling it's all hopeless. I shouldn't care to die believing *that*.

KAARLO

Then you won't die believing it's hopeless. That's the point, my friend. You have lived in faith—the light is in you—and it is the light which gives the strength that defeats death. It's only the fearful—the unbelieving—those who have sold themselves to the murderers and the liars—they are the only ones who can really die.

FRANK

But how can you deny that the light is going out —it's going fast—everywhere?

KAARLO (*with a growing sense of excitement*)

It is just beginning to burn with a healthy flame. I know this, because I have seen it. I have seen it in all kinds of men, of all races, and all varieties of faith. They are coming to consciousness. Look at all the millions of men now under arms, and all those that are fearful that arms may be thrust upon them. Are there any illusions of glory among any of them? None whatever! Isn't that progress?

BEN

Far be it from me to argue, Doctor—but I can't see the difference whether men go to war because of illusions of glory, or just in a spirit of grim resignation.

KAARLO

There is all the difference. Because those illusions, when shattered, leave men hollow. When men
lose their illusions, they say, "Oh, what's the use?
What have we got to live for?" They are devital-
ized by the conviction of futility. But grim resignation, as you call it, that makes a man say, "This
is an evil job—but I have to do it." And when men
say that, they are already beginning to ask, "But
why do I have to do it? *Why* must this evil go on
forever?" And when men start asking questions,
they are not satisfied until they find the answers.
That is consciousness. And for the first time in
history, consciousness is not just the privilege of
a few secluded philosophers. It is free for all. For
the first time, individual men are fighting to know
themselves. . . . Forgive me, gentlemen. I forget
myself. I think I am lecturing at the Medical Institute. But— (*He pauses to listen to the guns*)
—the Russians are only a short distance away.
This may be my last lecture. So—please permit
me to finish. . . . Listen! What you hear now—
this terrible sound that fills the earth—it is the
death rattle. One may say easily and dramatically
that it is the death rattle of civilization. But—I
choose to believe differently. I believe it is the long
deferred death rattle of the primordial beast. We
have within ourselves the power to conquer bestial-
ity, not with our muscles and our swords, but with
the power of the light that is in our minds. What a
thrilling challenge this is to all Science! To play

its part in the ultimate triumph of evolution. To help speed the day when man becomes genuinely human, instead of the synthetic creature—part bogus angel, part actual brute—that he has imagined himself in the dark past——

(*The sound of an approaching motorcycle is heard.*)

Is that an aeroplane?

(*All the men listen, tensely.*)

GOSDEN

No. It's a motorbike.

(*The sound stops.*)

Just a despatch rider, I expect. Maybe it's orders.

(JOE BURNETT *comes in from the left.*)

JOE

Hello, Ben. Hello, Frank. Hello, Doctor Valkonen.

FRANK

Joe!

BEN

Where did *you* drop from?

JOE

I saw Major Rutkowski up the road. He said you were in here.

KAARLO

Mr. Burnett! I am delighted to see you. Are you flying on this front now?

Joe

I was—up till half an hour ago. I was shot down. First time that ever happened to me. I just managed to make a landing behind our lines. I got a motor-cycle and I'm going back to headquarters to see if they have any more planes.

Gosden

Were you scouting the Russian lines?

Joe

Yes.

Gosden

How do things look?

Joe

Not too good. They're bringing up everything.

Ben

Have you been in Helsinki lately, Joe?

Joe

Yes. I was there a few days ago.

Ben

Is Dave Corween still on the job?

Joe

Yes. He's still telling bed-time stories.

Kaarlo

And I hope you called at my house, Mr. Burnett? Did you see my wife?

JOE

No—I didn't. (*He braces himself and crosses to* KAARLO.) I—I don't know how to say it, Doctor Valkonen—although God knows I've said it so many times before—but—I want you to know that you have my sympathy.

KAARLO

Your sympathy? (KAARLO *looks at him with such intense questioning that* JOE *gulps*.) Why do I have your sympathy, Mr. Burnett?

JOE

You don't know about your son?

KAARLO

No. (*He looks levelly at* JOE.) He's dead?

JOE

Yes.

KAARLO

Killed in action?

JOE

I believe he died in hospital, of wounds.

KAARLO

When was this?

JOE

I don't quite know. I heard of it only from Dave. He had seen Mrs. Valkonen.

KAARLO

Is—my wife well?

JOE

Yes, Doctor. She told Dave that she had been with your son in the hospital. He was married there, to Miss Alquist, before he died. His wife has gone to America. . . . I—I didn't know, Doctor, that I should be the bearer of this news— (*His voice trails off.*)

GOSDEN (*rising, and speaking with great diffidence.*)

I should like, sir, to be permitted to put in my word of sympathy, too.

BEN

And mine also, Doctor.

FRANK (*rising*)

Wouldn't you like us to get out of here, Doctor Valkonen?

KAARLO

No, no. Thank you. And thank you for telling me, Mr. Burnett. I imagine my wife has written me all this, but we have moved about so much that there have been no letters in weeks. I'm sorry you had to undergo this embarrassment.

(RUTKOWSKI *comes in. He carries a cartridge belt with a revolver in a holster.*)

RUTKOWSKI

I found the commanding officer. The Russians have occupied all the islands around Uuras. They're bringing tanks over the ice, and they're

going to attack in force here. The Finns are forming up to drive them back. They need more men.
They seem to be organizing the defense very well.
But they have no reserves. They need more men.
There's no point in trying to organize a field
ambulance station here, Doctor. I brought this
revolver and belt for you. It was salvaged from
some officer who was killed. There are rifles for
you men to use.

(*He hands the belt and holster to* KAARLO,
who takes out the revolver and stares at it.)

FRANK

We're to fight?

RUTKOWSKI

There's no compulsion if you don't wish to go.

JOE (*quietly*)

I'll be glad to go, Major.

BEN

So will I.

RUTKOWSKI (*to* JOE)

Not you, Lieutenant. If there are any planes
left, we need them in the air. You will report back
to headquarters at Sakkijaarvi.

JOE (*resigned*)

Very good, sir.

KAARLO

We must go now? At once?

RUTKOWSKI

We may as well wait here for a little while.
There will be plenty of warning when the attack
starts.

KAARLO

Then—I would like to write a letter. (*He puts
the revolver and belt down on the desk.*) Perhaps
you will take it with you, Mr. Burnett? There
must be some way that they could send it on to
Helsinki.

JOE

I'll do everything I possibly can, Doctor Valkonen.

KAARLO (*to* RUTKOWSKI)

If I'm not finished when you're ready to go, just
call me.

RUTKOWSKI

I will, Doctor.

(KAARLO *goes out at the right, taking his foun-
tain pen from his pocket.*)

Have any of you gentlemen a cigarette?

(BEN *hands him one.*)

Thank you. . . . I suppose Doctor Valkonen wants
to write his valedictory.

JOE

It isn't that, Major. I just gave him the news
that his son was killed.

RUTKOWSKI

Oh—when I came in—I saw his face—but I didn't
know the explanation. (*He lights his cigarette,*

being careful to mask the flame with his great-coat.)

FRANK (*with sudden vehemence*)

Do you know that Doctor Valkonen believes in the teachings of Christ? He believes in them as if they were scientific facts, which can yet be proved. He says so in his book. He says you can't resist evil by building Maginot Lines and big navies. The true defenses of man are *in* man, himself. . . . So now—there's nothing left for that great thinker to do but take a gun and go up there and shoot. (*He has crossed above the desks and looks at the revolver.*)

BEN

And how about you, Frank? Are you going up? What does the old conscience say?

FRANK

What the hell do you think it says? How could I ever live with myself again if I didn't go? That's what happens when you expose yourself to this. Oh, God—how many times have I taken an oath that if the United States were ever again duped into going to war, I'll be a conscientious objector! Let them put me in Leavenworth. I'd rather be there. I'd consider it takes more courage to be there than in the front line. But—here's the choice —given to me now—and I haven't got the guts to say, "No—I won't fight."

(*He has crossed to the left and sits down on the floor beside* JOE. RUTKOWSKI *is sitting on the cen-*

ter desk. The others are seated at the other desks.)

BEN

Why don't you put all that into a poem, Frank?

FRANK

All right, Ben—go ahead and kid me.

BEN

I don't feel in a position to kid you, Frank. I've had a few necessary changes of heart myself. Once I lost a good job because they decided I was a Red. Yes. I've spent hours arguing that the Soviet Union is the greatest sociological advance in history—the greatest force for peace on earth today. . . . Now—go ahead and kid *me!*

RUTKOWSKI (*bitterly*)

Nobody is responsible for his opinions now. There *are* no opinions on anything.

GOSDEN (*to* RUTKOWSKI)

How do our positions look in the line, sir?

RUTKOWSKI

Fairly well placed.

GOSDEN

Do you think we would have any chance of holding them?

RUTKOWSKI (*with no emotion*)

No—I don't think so.

BEN (*with a nervous laugh*)

I take it, Major—you feel we're all condemned to death?

RUTKOWSKI

Yes.

(BEN *stands up. He is whistling.*)

BEN

I can't help agreeing with you, Frank. It seems a silly way to end your life.

JOE

Any way is silly. A cousin of mine was killed—he and his girl both—driving home from a debutante party at the Ritz in New York. He was a little tight, and he didn't notice the Dead End sign —and—phft!—right into the East River!

FRANK

And is that any reason why we should fight—and die?

GOSDEN (*to* FRANK)

Every one of us can find plenty of reasons for *not* fighting, and they're the best reasons in the world. But—the time comes when you've bloody well got to fight—and you might just as well go cheerfully.

FRANK (*rising to his knees*)

Cheerful! What are you, anyway? Are you so stupid you can't even *think?* You said you have a

wife and two little children in England. Aren't
you giving any thought to them now?

GOSDEN (*in a choked voice*)

I'll have to ask you not to mention them. My
people know what I'm doing—and why.

FRANK (*sinking back on his heels*)

Excuse me.

RUTKOWSKI (*looking off toward the left*)

Poor Doctor Valkonen. He is a philosopher.
He is also, for some strange reason, an optimist.
He will be better dead.

BEN

Why do you say that, Major?

RUTKOWSKI

Perhaps it is only because I am Polish. (*He looks
levelly at* FRANK.) You asked this gentleman to
give a thought to his wife and children in England.
He can think of them happily. My wife—my baby
—my father—and mother—are in Warsaw—or they
were there, when the Nazis came. My wife is twenty-four years old. She is very beautiful. She is
the most beautiful person I have ever known. And
I have read in Cardinal Hlond's report, that he
has sent to the Pope—I have read that the good-
looking women and the girls in Poland have been
sent into Germany to be whores. (*He rises quickly
and raps at the door at the right. He turns to the
others.*) Well!

GOSDEN (*in a desperate effort to change the subject*)

I wish I'd thought to write a line myself. I *did* think of it—but I didn't know what to say. I wish I'd written to my missus to tell her I'm going up the line in good company.

(KAARLO *comes in from the right. He is sealing the envelope.* BEN *slaps* GOSDEN *on the back.*)

KAARLO

Here you are, Mr. Burnett.

(JOE *crosses and gets the letter from* KAARLO.)

JOE

I'm sure it will be delivered safely.

(*He shakes hands with* KAARLO, *and salutes* RUTKOWSKI, *who returns the salute.*)

KAARLO

.Thank you so much.

JOE

Good-bye, sir.

(GOSDEN *picks up his coat and rifle. All are now making preparations to go.* KAARLO *goes to the desk to get the belt and revolver and put them on.*)

GOSDEN (*to* JOE)

Best of luck, mate.

JOE

Same to you.

(GOSDEN *goes out.* JOE *is about to go.*)

Ben

Joe, if you ever get back, I wish you'd send a word to my mother, Mrs. Bessie Gichner—Cincinnati. You can get her address at the American Express Company's main office in New York. They all know me there.

Joe (*as* Ben *goes out*)

I'll remember that, Ben . . . (*He starts out.*) If I get back——

Frank

Hey, Joe—wait a minute. I've got a message, too!

(Joe *and* Frank *have gone out on this.* Rutkowski *has been watching* Kaarlo *with silent sympathy as he puts on the belt.*)

Rutkowski

Forgive me, Doctor Valkonen. I hadn't known of the great loss you have suffered.

Kaarlo

Thank you. I had been expecting that news for a long time. I was prepared for it. My son had a good character—part Finnish, part American. He was not afraid.

(*He starts to go.* Rutkowski *is by the door at the left.*)

Rutkowski

Doctor, I think you had better take off that Red Cross arm band.

(RUTKOWSKI *goes. It is now so dark that*
KAARLO *is a silhouette as he rips off the Red Cross*
arm band. He goes out. The sound of the guns
increases.)

CURTAIN

SCENE VII

The Valkonens' living room. The only noticeable difference in the room is that all the autographed photographs have been removed from their frames.

Uncle Waldemar *is at a window, looking out. It is a beautiful, sunny day.*

After a moment, Dave *and* Joe *come in from the dining room.* Uncle Waldemar *turns quickly.*

Uncle Waldemar
I was enjoying the beautiful day.

Dave
It *is* beautiful. It's beginning to feel almost like spring.

Uncle Waldemar
Did you have a nice lunch?

Dave
Wonderful, thank you.

Uncle Waldemar
I'll go help Miranda clear the dishes.

Dave
We begged to be allowed to help, but were ordered out of the kitchen.

167

UNCLE WALDEMAR

Of course. (*He gives them a courtly bow.*) You are guests.

(*He goes out.* DAVE *offers* JOE *a cigarette.*)

DAVE

An incredible display of stoicism.

JOE

God—I didn't know what to say. I never know what to say. Anything you can think of sounds so lame.

DAVE

You didn't need to say anything, Joe. She's lost everybody that she loves—and now she's in terrible danger of losing her own life. But it's a matter of principle that neither she nor any one else must ever admit that there are certain undertones of tragedy in the situation. After all the centuries, New England is still New England. You might even go so far as to say that it's still England. Keeping a stiff upper lip.

JOE

How long do you figure it will take the Russians to get here?

DAVE

I don't know. But I suspect it won't be long. Berlin has given out orders that this little incident must end—and if the Russians don't hurry, there are going to be some serious tantrums in the Wilhelmstrasse.

JOE

This city might hold out for a long time, like Madrid.

DAVE

I hope not. Because if it comes to a siege, you'll see German battleships out there, doing their bit in the bombardment. I wouldn't like to be here when that happens. I saw them at Danzig when they were battering Westerplatte. I could see the Nazis, watching their own barrage. They were deriving a sexual thrill from that display of devastating power.

JOE

What happens to you when you get caught in a captured city?

DAVE

I know how to wave my little red passport. I can say "I'm an American journalist" in all languages. In Nanking, I had to say it in Japanese. Oh—I get pushed around a bit—but I always live to broadcast the final hours of another gallant little republic. . . . But what about you, Joe? Have you got a plane?

JOE

I don't know. I may be in the army now. It would be pretty humiliating to end my career in the god-damned infantry.

DAVE (*looking toward the kitchen*)
That's what Doctor Valkonen did.
(JOE *also glances toward the kitchen.*)

JOE

Listen, Dave—can't you get Mrs. Valkonen out of this—and the old man, too?

DAVE

I've tried—but they won't leave. They're going to wait here for whatever comes, the Russians, or the Nazis, or both. They've even planned how they'll burn the house down. That's required by Finnish tradition. It's like the scorched earth in China. Mrs. Valkonen wants to stay here and die, just as her husband did. She doesn't care what happens.

JOE

It's a pity.

DAVE

That's just what it is, Joe. A wholesale pity. Three months ago, the Soviet troops marched in. They had brass bands and truck-loads of propaganda with them. They thought it would be a grand parade through Finland, like May Day in the Red Square. So now—several hundred thousand men have been killed—millions of lives have been ruined. The cause of revolution all over the world has been set back incalculably. The Soviet Union has been reduced from the status of a great power to that of a great fraud. And the Nazis have won another bloodless victory.

(MIRANDA *and* UNCLE WALDEMAR *come in from the kitchen.* MIRANDA *wears an apron, but her*

dress is, as always, very feminine and chic. DAVE
and JOE *rise.)*

MIRANDA

Well—we've washed all the dishes and put them
away neatly, and now Uncle Waldemar and I
haven't a thing to do until supper. Sit down,
Dave—Mr. Burnett.

JOE

I'm sorry, Mrs. Valkonen. I have to go and
report for duty, whatever it is.

MIRANDA

Oh—I'm sorry. But thank you so much for coming, and bringing the letter, and telling me all
about that little schoolhouse.

JOE

I—I'm glad I could get here. You've been very
kind to me. I can tell you that—I won't ever forget you, or Doctor Valkonen. . . . Good-bye, Mr.
Sederstrum. (*He shakes hands with* UNCLE
WALDEMAR.) Good-bye, Dave—I'll probably be
seeing you. (*He shakes hands with* DAVE.)

DAVE

Yes, Joe—good-bye.

JOE

And if you get home before I do, don't forget
those messages for Ben's and Frank's families.

DAVE

I won't, Joe.

MIRANDA

I wish you the very best of luck, Mr. Burnett.

JOE

You needn't worry about me, Mrs. Valkonen. The beautiful part of my life is that it's so utterly worthless nobody bothers to deprive me of it. Good-bye. (*He goes out at the right.*)

MIRANDA

I hope he comes through all right. He's the only one left of those young men who went to Viipuri with Kaarlo . . . I suppose you'll be going soon, Dave?

DAVE

I'm not sure, Mrs. Valkonen. There's some talk of their sending me to Stockholm. They want to investigate those peace rumors.

MIRANDA

Do you think there might be peace before the Russians get here to Helsinki?

DAVE

I hope so.

UNCLE WALDEMAR (*in a completely matter-of-fact tone*)

It doesn't make much difference. Either the war continues and we suffer the fate of Poland, or peace comes, as it did at Munich, and we become

another Czechoslovakia. In any case, we live
only at the mercy of the enemy.

MIRANDA

You'll have a great book to write about all this
—won't you, Dave? Your own personal history.

DAVE

I'm afraid that words will fail me, Mrs. Valkonen. Just as they've failed the whole human
race.

MIRANDA

I'd like to read your book, Dave.

DAVE (*he looks at her*)

What are you going to do, Mrs. Valkonen?
Are you—are you planning just to sit here and
wait for them?

MIRANDA

Oh no, we have our plans all made. Get out the
guns, Uncle Waldemar.

(UNCLE WALDEMAR *goes out at the right.*)

DAVE

Guns?

MIRANDA

We got them at the hospital. They'd been
discarded by wounded soldiers. Uncle Waldemar
and I have been practicing—not shooting, of
course; but just learning how to work them. When
this war started, Dave—when the Russians first

attacked us—the President said we would fight—
even the women, and the old people, and the children would fight. We have no children here—only
that one in Boston, who is unborn. But Uncle
Waldemar and I are here.

(UNCLE WALDEMAR *returns with two army
rifles and some cartridge belts.*)

When we see them coming from the shore down
there, we'll light the fire. It's all ready, down in
the cellar. Then we'll go out into the garden, behind the stone wall, with the guns and ammunition.
(*She takes one of the rifles and a clip of ammunition.*) You see—you put the clip in like this—
then you shove the bolt. (*She shoves it with a
snap.*) After each shot, you twist it and pull it
back, to throw out the empty shell. Like this . . .
(*She demonstrates, manipulating the bolt. The
shells fly out.*) What do you think of that, Dave?
(*She looks up at the 1812 portrait.*) Great-
grandfather Eustis thinks it's fine!

(*There is something maniacal in this statement.
She puts the gun against the wall and picks up a
parcel from the piano.*)

I hate to add to your burdens as a carrier of bad
news, Dave. But—I have a package here, that I
want you to take, and also a letter from Kaarlo—
the one he wrote in the schoolhouse before he was
killed. The package contains Kaarlo's signed pictures of Freud and Pavlov and Carrel and the
Mayos. He was very proud of those pictures.

There's also the Nobel gold medal. I want you to take the package and the letter and give them to Kaatri, to keep for her child. You have that address in Boston—my aunt, who is going to pay you back the fifty dollars I borrowed?

DAVE

Yes. I have the address.

MIRANDA (*looking at the letter*)

Kaarlo had just heard from me about Erik's death. He wanted to comfort me, in his curious way. Do you mind if I read you the letter?

DAVE

Please do, Mrs. Valkonen.

MIRANDA (*reading*)

"In this time of our own grief it is not easy to summon up the philosophy which has been formed from long study of the sufferings of others. But I must do it, and you must help me." You see—he wanted to make me feel that I'm stronger—wiser. "I have often read the words which Pericles spoke over the bodies of the dead, in the dark hour when the light of Athenian democracy was being extinguished by the Spartans. He told the mourning people that he could not give them any of the old words which tell how fair and noble it is to die in battle. Those empty words were old, even then, twenty-four centuries ago. But he urged them to find revival in the memory of the commonwealth which they together had achieved; and he promised them that the story of their commonwealth would never die, but would live on, far away, woven into the fabric of other men's lives. I believe that these words can be said now of our own dead, and our own commonwealth. I have always believed in the mystic truth of the resurrection. The great leaders of the mind and the spirit—Socrates, Christ, Lincoln—were all done to death that the full measure of their contribution to human experience might never be lost. Now—the death of our son is only a fragment in the death of our country. But Erik and the others who give their lives are also giving to mankind a symbol—a little symbol, to be sure, but a clear one—of man's unconquerable aspiration to dignity and freedom and purity in the sight of God. When I made that radio speech" —you remember? . . . "I quoted from St. Paul. I repeat those words to you now, darling: 'We glory in tribulations; knowing that tribulation worketh patience; and patience, experience; and experience, hope.' There are men here from all different countries. Fine men. Those Americans who were at our house on New Year's Day—and that nice Polish officer, Major Rutkowski—they are all here. They are waiting for me now, so I must close this, with all my love."

(*She folds the letter and hands it to* DAVE.) There it is, Dave. Take good care of it.

DAVE

I shall, Mrs. Valkonen. But it may be a long time before I can deliver it.

MIRANDA

It will be a long time before my grandchild learns to read.

DAVE (*after a moment's silence*)

I—I have to be going now . . . (*He goes quickly to* UNCLE WALDEMAR.) Good-bye, Mr. Sederstrum.

UNCLE WALDEMAR (*shaking hands with* DAVE)

Good-bye, Mr. Corween.

MIRANDA

You'll surely let us know if you're going to Stockholm?

DAVE

Oh, yes, Mrs. Valkonen.

MIRANDA

We'll miss you very much, Dave. You've really become part of our life here in Helsinki.

(MIRANDA *and* DAVE *have gone out on that.* UNCLE WALDEMAR *looks after them, then he sits down at the piano. Still looking toward the door, he starts to play the Finnish folk song heard at the end of the first scene. After a moment,* MIRANDA *returns. She goes to the couch, and sits down where she had sat beside* KAARLO. *She listens to* UNCLE WALDEMAR'S *playing. She looks to the left, where* ERIK *had been, and to the right, where* KAARLO *had been. She leans backward, wearily, and looks at nothing.* UNCLE WALDEMAR *goes on playing the tinkly little tune. There is a kind of peace in this Finnish-American house.*)

CURTAIN

THE END

BODY

BONES, MUSCLES, BLOOD, AND OTHER BODY BITS

BODY

BONES, MUSCLES, BLOOD, AND OTHER BODY BITS

By
Richard Walker

Consultant
Dr. Gabrielle Murphy

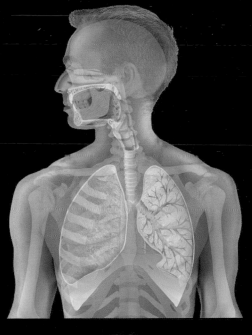

A Dorling Kindersley Book

LONDON, NEW YORK, SYDNEY, DELHI,
PARIS, MUNICH, and JOHANNESBURG

Editor Lucy Hurst
Art Editor Ann Cannings
Senior Editor Fran Jones
Senior Art Editor Marcus James
Category Publisher Jayne Parsons
Managing Art Editor Jacquie Gulliver
US Editors Gary Werner and
Margaret Parrish
Picture Researcher Brenda Clynch
DK Pictures Rachel Holt
Production Erica Rosen
DTP Designers Matthew Ibbotson and
Louise Paddick

First American Edition, 2001

01 02 03 04 05 10 9 8 7 6 5 4 3 2 1

Published in the United States by
DK Publishing, Inc.
95 Madison Avenue
New York, New York 10016

CIP data is available from the Library of Congress.

ISBN 0-7894-7967-2 (hc)
ISBN 0-7894-7968-0 (pb)

Reproduced by Colourscan, Singapore
Printed and bound by L.E.G.O., Italy

See our complete catalog at

www.dk.com

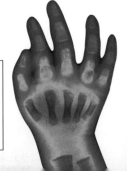

CONTENTS

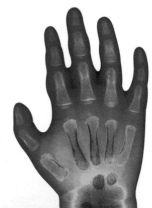

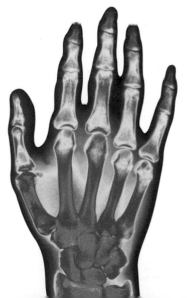

INTRODUCTION

Wherever we live, whatever we do, we all share one thing in common. A body! But, is that a reason to take our bodies for granted? Certainly not! The inside story of the human body is altogether too exciting, gruesome, and entertaining to be ignored.

And what a story it is — pieced together over many centuries by doctors, scientists, and others who were fascinated by what bodies are made of and how they work. Thanks to their efforts we now understand that the body's component parts — better known as systems — each have their own role. Put all these systems together, and you will understand the human body.

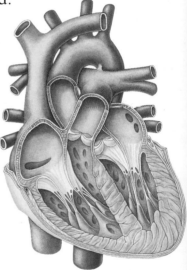

THE HEART CONSTANTLY PUMPS BLOOD AROUND YOUR BODY.

You'll find out what keeps your body upright and why it moves when you want it to. All will be revealed about the mysteries of the brain, as well as why skunks smell so unpleasant. Read on, and you'll discover how you take in life-giving oxygen, get energy from your food, as well as how urine is made or what the liver does. All this against a background of the heart pumping blood to every one of the body's cells. And there's more. You'll meet grave-robbing body snatchers, a railroad worker with an iron rod through his head, Frankenstein's monster, and other fascinating characters who have all affected our knowledge of the human body.

Having found out about the body's parts, there's also time to investigate the living overcoat of protective skin that holds them all together. Not to mention the committed body defense and repair service that springs into action if anything goes wrong.

And, if this wasn't enough, we also have the means to reproduce and make new human beings to take over when our life is completed.

And there you have it – a walking, talking, breathing human body. For those of you who want to explore the subject in more detail, there are black "Log On" boxes that appear throughout the book. These will direct you to some fascinating websites where you can check out even more.

MUSCLES AND BONES SUPPORT AND MOVE YOUR BODY.

Richard Walker.

BODY BASICS

There's no doubt that we human beings are the most intelligent animals on planet Earth. We're also very curious, constantly wanting to explore the world around us, including finding out about our own bodies. We have come to understand its basic workings – right down to the tiniest cell – through a process of detective work that stretches back to our earliest ancestors.

ANCESTORS OF ALL MODERN HUMANS LIVED IN AFRICA

Early humans
Even as far back as 30,000 years ago, we know that people were aware of their bodies. Early humans recorded images of the human body as paintings on cave walls and in simple sculptures.

They were able to use their hands to paint, mold, or carve because, millions of years

before, the earliest humans – such as Australopithecus – had already switched from moving on all fours like their ape cousins, to standing upright on two legs. This left their hands free to do all kinds of things.

Your closest living non-human relative today – the bonobo chimpanzee – descends from a branch of the human-ape family that didn't make the move to two legs.

ONE OF THE EARLIEST HUMANS WAS AUSTRALOPITHECUS.

Same or different?

If you walk down the street today, it won't take you long to realize that human bodies come in all shapes, sizes, and skin colors. Humans, like most animals, also fall into two distinct groups – females and males.

Despite these differences, all human bodies have the same basic anatomy – or structure – and work in exactly the same way, except for the parts that make us male or female. We know about anatomy because of all the body information that has been pieced together over thousands of years. Each culture has had its own individual ideas about what made the human body tick.

Early views

The ancient Greeks, for example, thought there were four "humors" in the body – blood, yellow bile, black bile,

THESE KIDS LOOK DIFFERENT, BUT THEIR ANATOMY IS THE SAME.

and phlegm. Any imbalance in these humors would make someone ill. Especially someone with no sense of humor!

Claudius Galen (AD 129–201), a Greek doctor, adopted these ideas and became a star physician in Rome. There was a ban, unfortunately, on dissecting (cutting up) humans, so he used pigs, goats, and sheep, assuming that their anatomy would be the same. It wasn't! But Galen was so convincing that everyone accepted his ideas, many of which were wrong.

After his death, Galen's views about the body remained unchallenged for more than 1,300 years. People who dared to criticize Galen's books were either laughed at or punished.

THE FOUR HUMORS

PHLEGM

BLOOD

BLACK BILE

YELLOW BILE

New ideas

By the 16th century, however, Galen's beliefs were starting to be questioned. Two people – Leonardo da Vinci (1452–1519) and Andreas Vesalius (1514–64) – played a key part in waving goodbye to the past.

Leonardo was a brilliant artist and scientist. He dissected more than 30 bodies by candlelight in the Santo Spirito mortuary. Using his own – not Galen's – observations and incredible technical skills, Leonardo drew what he actually saw in a thousand accurate drawings of the body.

Vesalius, a doctor, was tired of other doctors pretending not to notice that the insides of bodies looked nothing like the pictures in dusty old books. So he started stealing the bodies of executed criminals, taking them home, and cutting them up to see how they were put together. Some bodies were kept for weeks, so he must have had understanding neighbors!

In 1543 Vesalius published his notes in a book called *De Humanis Corporis Fabrica* which, for those of you who don't read Latin, means *The Structure of the*

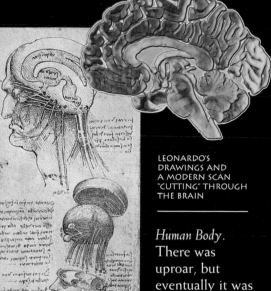

LEONARDO'S DRAWINGS AND A MODERN SCAN "CUTTING" THROUGH THE BRAIN

Human Body. There was uproar, but eventually it was realized that Vesalius was right and Galen was wrong.

Body snatchers

In 16th-century England, doctors wanting to find out about, or teach, anatomy were only allowed to use the bodies of executed criminals. But the sudden interest in anatomy meant that the supply of dead bodies just couldn't keep up with demand.

It didn't take long for some bright person to realize that there was money to be made in selling dead bodies to unscrupulous doctors. Gangs of "body snatchers" would dig up freshly buried corpses from graveyards and deliver them to medical schools in return for cash.

In the 1820s, two Scottish body snatchers were getting tired of digging up bodies. William Burke and William Hare decided to murder people instead, supplying fresh corpses to their doctor client. It wasn't long before they were caught. Hare betrayed Burke, who was hanged and his body was sent for dissection!

Seeing inside a body

Until the end of the 19th century, the best way that doctors could see inside the body – living or dead – was to cut it open. But in 1895, things changed. German scientist

Wilhelm Roentgen found that X-rays could pass through soft things, like skin and muscle, but not hard materials, like bones. He shook up the medical world when he discovered that, by projecting X-rays through the body onto photographic film, he could produce a picture of the inside of the body showing bones but not soft tissues. Doctors could now see fractures, and weird things like bullets and swallowed coins.

More high-tech methods were invented in the 1970s and '80s. One of them, called MRI (magnetic resonance imaging), combines magnetism and radiowaves to produce "slices" through the body without spilling a drop of blood. Another, called ultrasound, bounces sound waves off body parts and uses the echo to make a picture of what's happening inside. Because it is very safe,

BODY SNATCHERS AT WORK

ultrasound is used to check how a baby is getting along as it grows inside its mother.

Cells, tissues, and organs

It's all very well to be able to accurately describe the parts of the body. But what is each part actually made of? Dutchman Antoni van Leeuwenhoek (1632 1723) found the answer when he designed a simple microscope, and discovered minute living units inside the body – cells.

Your body is made up of not millions, not billions, but trillions of cells. In total there are about 200 different types of cell including blood cells, bone cells, and brain cells. Cells with the same task work together to make tissues, such as muscles that allow you to move. Different types of tissues cooperate to form organs, like the stomach or brain Organs with linked roles make up a system, like the digestive system which processes your lunch. Altogether, 12 systems fit together to make up your body.

THIS MRI SCAN SHOWS THE ORGANS
AND BONES INSIDE THE BODY

MEAT AND BONES

Without its supporting skeleton, the body would be as useful as a tent without poles. In other words, you would be spread out on the ground unable to find the remote control! To work properly, bones need meat, or muscles. Hundreds of skeletal muscles pull on your bones so you can walk, write, and do thousands of other things. Between them, muscles and bones shape, support, and move your body.

HALF MUSCLE, HALF BONE

BY WEIGHT, BONE IS STRONGER THAN STEEL

Bony frame

Did you know that your skeleton has 206 bones? Some of them are tiny, like the rice grain-sized stirrup bone deep inside your ear. Others, like the mighty femur in your thigh, are big and strong enough to carry your weight. Inside your flexible but strong bony framework, soft organs like the brain and heart are protected from damage.

14

LOG ON...
www.last-word.com/
lastword/body.html

Your bones also provide somewhere to anchor muscles, so that you can tug on them and make your body jump, dance, and run when you want it to.

What bones are made of
People often think of bones as being dry, dusty, and dead, because that is how we usually see them. But bones inside a living person are nothing like that. They are one-third water, full of nerves and blood vessels, and contain cells that are forever rebuilding and reshaping your bones. Living bones are made of mineral salts for hardness, and collagen fibers for strength. After death, the collagen rots away leaving just a hard but brittle bone-shaped shell behind.

For a closer look inside bones, you would need a microscope. This would show that bones are made up of different parts. The outer layer of bone has tubes of bony tissue running along it – like rolled-up newspaper – that give it strength. Because they are crammed together these tubes are called compact bone.

Further inside, bone looks like honeycomb. Struts and spaces make this spongy bone strong but light. If your bones weren't spongy, they would be so heavy you wouldn't be able to move your body.

BLOOD VESSELS AND
NERVES INSIDE
LIVING BONE

WHEN A PERSON DOES YOGA, IT HELPS TO MAKE THEIR JOINTS MORE FLEXIBLE.

Blood factory

As well as supporting you, bones also make the red blood cells that whizz around your body. The blood cell factory is found in bone marrow, the jellylike stuff inside bones. There are two types of marrow. Fatty, yellow marrow – much loved by dogs when they chew bones – doesn't make blood cells. But red marrow – found inside your shoulder blades, ribs, breastbone, and pelvis – does. The high-speed red

EVERY SECOND, BONE MARROW MAKES 2,000,000 RED BLOOD CELLS

It may seem a bit odd, but when you were much younger and smaller you had more bones in your skeleton than you do now. A newborn baby has more than 300 "bones" making up its skeleton. In fact, some of these "bones" aren't very hard. They are made of cartilage, the stuff that makes your nose and ears bendable. Then as you get older, real bone replaces cartilage to make your bones longer and stronger. And some bones join together. That's why you've ended up with fewer than you started with.

marrow production line churns out exactly the right number of red blood cells needed to replace the worn-out ones.

THESE HAND X-RAYS SHOW HOW BONES (PURPLE) REPLACE CARTILAGE BY THE TIME YOU ARE AN ADULT.

HAND OF A
ONE-YEAR-OLD

Moving joints

Pick up your favorite food item and, without bending your arm at all, pop it into your mouth. Impossible, isn't it? So, thank goodness for joints – the bendable points in the skeleton where bones meet and make movement possible. Some joints, like those in the hip and shoulder, allow all-around movement. Others, like the hinge joint in the knee, only allow movement back and forth. To stop lots of grinding noises when you move, most joints have thick, oily liquid inside which makes them work smoothly, like a well-oiled machine.

The skull has a different kind of joint. Press your fingers against the sides of your head.

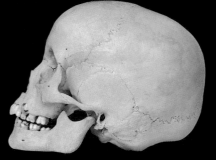

THE SUTURES IN THIS SIX-YEAR-OLD'S SKULL FIT TOGETHER LIKE A JIGSAW.

You should find – unless you're an alien – that you can't squeeze it inward. That's because, although your skull is made up of 22 separate bones, the joints between them don't move. Sutures, as these joints are called, fit tightly together

HAND OF A
20-YEAR-OLD

HAND OF A
THREE-YEAR-OLD

they pop out of their joints and tear their ligaments – the shoulder is a common place for this to happen. Doctors call this dislocation and it needs their expert skills to carefully maneuver the bones back into place without too much nerve pinching or tissue crunching. Ouch!

Handy hands

So, if you put all this together, you can see how important your bones, joints, and ligaments are. Your hands are a good example. Ever since our hairy ancestors moved from walking on four legs to two, humans have had their hands free to do all kinds of things. Writing a letter or lifting a heavy weight are only two of the many tasks your hands can perform. Why are they so versatile?

like jigsaw pieces. This makes the skull really strong, ideal for protecting your squishy brain and giving your face its shape. In fact, there is one skull bone – the lower jaw – that does move. This is fortunate, otherwise you wouldn't be able to open your mouth to eat your lunch.

While joints may be great for making the skeleton flexible, without ligaments they would be useless. Ligaments are strong – but slightly elastic – straps that hold bones together at joints, like in the knee. They stop bones from moving too much or in the wrong directions. Sometimes, if you push your bones too far,

• Each hand is made of 27 small bones, making it very flexible.

• Your thumb can touch the tips of the other four fingers.

• Some 20 muscles in the forearm pull on hand bones. They do this by using long tendons (you can see them on the back of the hand or under the wrist), to produce hundreds of different types

LIGAMENTS (BROWN) AROUND THE KNEE JOINT HOLD IT TOGETHER.

of movements, from a powerful grip to the most delicate touch.

Because your bones remain behind after you are long gone, people have always been able to see what a skeleton looks like. But finding out about muscles was a more gruesome task until recently. Let's see how it was done.

S how us your muscles! You wouldn't have wanted to be a criminal centuries ago, or you might have been flayed! This messy process involved carefully cutting away a person's skin to expose

THE WORD "MUSCLE" COMES FROM EARLY ROMANS WHO BELIEVED A CONTRACTING MUSCLE LOOKED LIKE A LITTLE MOUSE – "MUSCULUS" – RUNNING AROUND UNDER THE SKIN.

the muscles underneath. This was useful to doctors trying to teach their students how muscles worked.

So what is muscle made of? Muscle is made up of cells called fibers. Unlike most body cells, they are not small and compact, but instead, are long and packed with special stringy filaments. These filaments work together to make the muscle fiber contract, or get shorter.

WAX MODEL, MADE IN 1785 IN ITALY, SHOWS THE MUSCLES OF THE UPPER BODY.

They do this when your brain – which is the boss – says so, by sending nerve signals. If the fibers in a muscle contract, the whole muscle gets shorter, and that part of the body moves.

Meat market

To imagine what your muscles look like, take a trip to the meat counter at your local supermarket – vegetarians beware! Those red chunks of meat are the skeletal muscles of sheep, cows, and other animals. The "meat" from your own body makes up more than 40 percent of your body weight.

ACHILLES' MOM DIPPING HIM INTO THE STYX RIVER TO TRY AND MAKE HIM IMMORTAL.

TRICEPS   BICEPS

TRICEPS AND BICEPS WORK TOGETHER TO MOVE YOUR ARM UP AND DOWN.

Tendons

Just above your heel, at the back of your leg, you should be able to feel a fairly solid ridge of tissue. That's your Achilles tendon. Like other tendons, it's a tough cord that links muscles to bones.

Achilles was a Greek hero. When he was young, his mother held him by the heel and dipped him into the Styx River to make him immortal. This worked well until he was shot in his undipped heel with an arrow and died. From this sad tale we get the name Achilles tendon. Through it, the calf muscles pull on the ankle bone to point the foot downward.

Push and pull muscles

Pulling may be a specialty of muscles, but pushing certainly

20

isn't. Muscle fibers use energy to contract, but then they just relax to return to their normal length. So, if you want to bend and straighten your arm, for example, you need at least two muscles: one (the biceps) to pull the bones one way to bend, and one (the triceps) to pull the other way and straighten. This arrangement of muscles is found all over your body. Some pull bones one way, and others in the opposite direction.

A number of muscles work all the time that you are awake. Those in your back, neck, and buttocks, for example, stay partially contracted to hold you upright and give you posture. This muscle tone, as it is known, disappears when you fall asleep. That's why a sleeping body gets all floppy.

Making faces
Wherever you go in the world a smile means the same thing. So does a frown for that matter. More than 20 small muscles around the eyes, nose, and mouth produce the facial expressions that show when you are happy or annoyed or, for that matter, frightened, sad, angry, surprised, or disgusted.

Facial muscles are a little unusual because instead of pulling on bones, they tug at the skin on your face. Just a tiny twitch can alter your facial expression to reveal a subtle change in mood. In fact, the only way to keep your feelings to yourself is to put a paper bag over your head!

THIS MAORI MAN'S FACIAL EXPRESSION SHOWS HE IS READY TO FIGHT.

WEIRD WORLD
TONGUES ARE MADE OF MUSCLE TOO. TONGUE MUSCLES MAKE IT THICKER, THINNER, LONGER, OR SHORTER AS WELL AS PULLING IT IN OR PUSHING IT OUT , HELPING YOU TO SPEAK, SWALLOW... OR LOOK AGGRESSIVE!

SENSATIONAL SENSES

At this very second, millions of tiny sensors are sending a stream of messages to your brain to tell it what's happening inside and outside your body. Touch sensors – they include pain, pressure, heat, and cold sensors too – are found all over the place. The other four senses – sight, hearing, taste, smell – have sensors inside special organs: the eyes, ears, tongue, and nose.

YOUR EYES CONTAIN 70 PERCENT OF YOUR BODY'S SENSORS

Vision on

Of all the senses, vision is probably the most important. It gives you a moving picture of the outside world. Being able to see means that you can read this book, find your way to the fridge, play soccer, and recognize your friends. To make vision happen, your eyes detect light, and your brain produces the pictures.

Like hollow golf balls, your eyes sit protected inside bony sockets in the skull. The inner lining of each eyeball is a thin layer called the retina that is packed with millions of light sensors. Light, reflected from things around you, zooms into the eye through the clear part at the front – the cornea which covers the iris and pupil – and is focused by the lens onto the retina. As light patterns hit the sensors they send signals to the back of your brain. Here the messages are

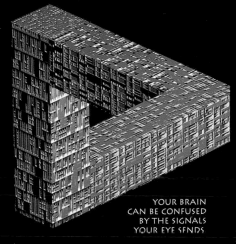

YOUR BRAIN CAN BE CONFUSED BY THE SIGNALS YOUR EYE SENDS

sorted out and you "see" what is in front of you.

Eye tricks

Your brain uses all kinds of clues to make pictures from the stream of signals sent from your eyes. But sometimes the clues aren't very clear, so the brain isn't really quite sure what to make of the

THE PUPIL GETS WIDER IN DIM LIGHT AND NARROWER IN BRIGHT LIGHT.

THE IRIS RANGES IN COLOR.

23

GLASSES HELP EYES FOCUS PROPERLY,
WHILE GLASS EYES REPLACE MISSING ONES.

are sent rippling through the air. These vibrations wobble their way into the inner ear where a snail shell-shaped thing called the cochlea sits.

Inside the cochlea are about 15,000 sound sensors, with lots of "hairs" sprouting from the top of them. As sound waves bounce in, they squash these hairs, and make the sensors send a message to

information it receives. This is how optical illusions happen. Your brain has been tricked!

Hear hear!

You may call those two floppy things on the side of your head ears, but in fact they're just one part of the sense organs that detect sounds. The main parts of the ears are hidden inside your skull bones. To find them you'd have to travel down the ear canal – the entrance is the hole in the middle of the floppy part or pinna – past the ear drum, over the tiny ear bones or ossicles, and into the inner ear.

When a baby cries, the orchestra tunes up, or your sister shouts at you, vibrations called sound waves

OPENING
OF THE
EAR CANAL

24

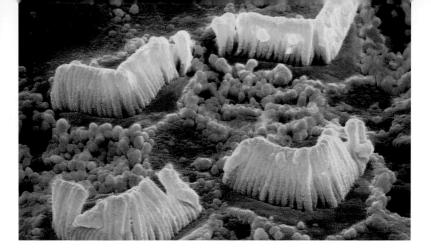

WHEN SOUND WAVES ENTER YOUR EAR,
THESE TINY HAIRS MOVE, CAUSING NERVES
TO CARRY A MESSAGE TO YOUR BRAIN.

OSSICLES   COCHLEA

EAR DRUM

your brain, via
nerves. Your brain is
so smart it can tell the
difference between a
high-pitched scream or
a low-pitched groan, the
loudness of a rock band, or
the quietness of a pin dropping.

B alanced view

Let's add an extra sense here,
that's related to hearing. That
sense is balance, the one that
stops you from
falling over and
tells you whether
you are standing on
your head, or not.
Sensors inside your
inner ear – next to
the cochlea – tell
your brain whether you
are moving forward,
backward, or
sideways, and
whether
you are
upright,
lying

MODEL SHOWING
INSIDE THE
HUMAN EAR

25

down, or upside down. With extra messages from your eyes, feet, and muscles, your brain gets enough information to tweak your muscles, move your body, and keep you balanced.

MOST PEOPLE WOULD FIND THIS VERY PAINFUL!

What a pain!

Although pain hurts, it's still a useful sensation. It's a warning signal that says your body may be injured. Of the three million pain sensors dotted around the body, most are in your skin. These skin sensors make you feel sharp pains, like when you prick your finger with a pin. Pain sensors inside your body produce longer-lasting aches like sore muscles or stomach cramps.

Stress can make the body produce its own natural pain-killers. That's why soldiers can be badly wounded in battle but feel nothing – until the fighting is over, and the painkillers wear off.

Touchy feely

Apart from pain detectors, there's a whole brigade of touch sensors in your skin. Some detect light touch, others vibrations, and yet others pick up different amounts of pressure. You can tell just by feeling the difference, for example, between velvet and sandpaper. Pressure sensors will let you know whether it's a friend standing on your foot, or an elephant (unless your best friend is an elephant!). And there's more. Grab a handful of ice cubes, and cold receptors soon let your brain know that your fingers are starting to freeze. Or, when you accidentally stick your foot in a bath that's too hot, heat sensors scream at you to pull your foot out before it cooks.

But, here's something

WEIRD WORLD
SOME PEOPLE WHO HAVE HAD A PART OF THEIR ARM OR LEG AMPUTATED CAN STILL FEEL PAIN OR ITCHING IN THE MISSING LIMB. THIS IS CALLED PHANTOM PAIN BECAUSE IT'S A GHOSTLY REMINDER OF WHAT USED TO BE THERE.

26

LOG ON...
www.KidsHealth.org/kid/

strange. Why is it that when you wear clothes they don't feel scratchy as they rub against your skin? You feel clothes as you put them on, but very quickly the sensation fades. Your brain just "ignores" the signals coming from the touch sensors in your skin. Scientists call this habituation. Without it, daily life would be very itchy and uncomfortable.

Good taste

Your tongue has touch sensors too (although fingers are better when you're feeling for that missing coin under the couch cushions.) It can detect heat – handy for preventing burning when you eat hot food – and has cold detectors, so you can feel the iciness of ice cream. It even has pain sensors. These can be triggered by a chemical in chile peppers called capsaicin. That's why chiles feel painfully hot. But, most important of all, your tongue can taste.

Look at your tongue in a mirror and you will see lots of tiny bumps, called papillae.

A MAGNIFIED VIEW OF THE SURFACE OF A TONGUE. TASTE BUDS SIT AT THE BASE OF THE BIG RED ROUND PAPILLAE.

Under the microscope some of these papillae look round, while some are pointed. About 10,000 taste buds – the sensors that detect tastes – are tucked under the sides of the round papillae. When you eat

adults can pick out 10,000 different odors, and children do even better. Smell works in the same basic way as taste. Breathe in through your nose, and odor molecules dissolve in the watery mucus (the stuff that

THE TONGUE DETECTS FOUR TASTES – SWEET, SOUR, SALTY, AND BITTER

something, taste molecules dissolve in saliva, and it's these that are picked up by the taste buds.

BITTER

SOUR, LIKE LEMONS

SALTY

SWEET

AREAS OF THE TONGUE RECOGNIZE DIFFERENT TASTES.

S mell this

When it comes to sensitivity, smell leaves taste far behind. It's an amazing 20,000 times more sensitive. What's more,

comes out when you sneeze) inside your nose. When these molecules hit smell detectors in the top of your nasal cavity – the space inside your nose – they fire off signals to the brain.

Smell and taste work together so that you can appreciate flavors. The nose is the boss in this partnership. If you have a blocked nose, food flavors become so bland that, blindfolded, you'd have problems telling what you are eating. Sometimes the two senses are in conflict, as people who eat durians soon discover. This southeast Asian fruit tastes simply delicious but smells like a public restroom on a hot day.

Apart from letting you appreciate the aromas of good food and fresh flowers, smell is useful in other ways. It helps you steer clear of stinking,

28

money on the phone bill!). Even more quirky is telekinesis, a feature of ESP that lets you move things just by thinking about it. But most scientists don't believe the evidence. They're sticking with five senses – for now!

rotten foods, and warns of possible dangers, such as smoke and burning. And if you get sprayed by a skunk, burn your clothes, and stay away from your friends for a week. Skunk spray contains mercaptan, the smelliest substance in the world. Humans can detect mercaptans when there is just one solitary molecule of the revolting stuff diluted in 30 billion molecules of air. Phew!

Five...or six?

So much for the five senses. But do you have an extra, sixth, sense? Well, some people think they do. Often called extrasensory perception or ESP, this mysterious sixth sense apparently allows you to use telepathy to read people's minds or to send them thoughts without speaking (that should save

SMELL DETECTORS SEND SIGNALS TO THE BRAIN AS YOU BREATHE IN.

TONGUE

SECTION THROUGH THE HEAD SHOWS TASTE AND SMELL SENSORY AREAS.

BRAIN POWER

What is pinky-gray, feels like a soft-boiled egg, and is as wrinkly as a walnut? It's your brain! It may seem incredible, but this wobbly mass is responsible for your personality and intelligence, your powers of communication, imagination, and memory, as well as controlling most body activities. Being soft makes the brain vulnerable, but luckily it sits well protected inside the bony dome of the skull.

STEVE MARTIN FELL IN LOVE WITH A BRAIN IN THE FILM "THE MAN WITH TWO BRAINS."

Protected brain
Your soft brain floats safely inside your skull, cushioned and nourished by a watery substance called cerebrospinal fluid. The fluid absorbs knocks that might otherwise damage the brain. But, this protection hasn't stopped curious people from investigating the brain. In the Stone Age, trepanning – as cutting skull holes is called – was done regularly. Exposing the brain was meant to cure headaches and mental illness.

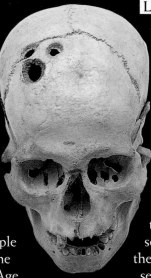

THE REMAINS OF A 4,000-YEAR-OLD TREPANNED SKULL

Left and right sides
Today, a lot more is understood about the brain. Its main section is the big wrinkly part called the cerebrum. Scientists have worked out that different parts of the cerebrum are involved in vision, hearing, movement, touch, speech, and so on. If you look at the cerebrum you can see that it is divided into two halves called the left and right cerebral hemispheres. The left hemisphere controls the right side of the body, and the right

30

hemisphere the left side. Usually the left hemisphere is dominant, which makes most people right-handed. The left hemisphere also controls speech, writing, numbers, and problem solving, while the right hemisphere deals with art, music, and recognizing faces.

Changed personality

The functions of the brain are also divided by area within each hemisphere. We know, for example, that the front of the brain is mostly responsible for personality because of

an accident involving Phineas Gage, a US railroad construction worker. In 1848, an explosion accidentally drove a 1 inch- (2.5 cm-) diameter iron bar through Gage's left cheek bone, the front of his brain, and then out through the top of his skull. Remarkably, Gage survived. But he became bad-tempered, lazy, and rude when before he had been a good worker and well-liked. His personality had completely

THE BRAIN, SEEN FROM ABOVE, SHOWS THE LEFT AND RIGHT SIDES OF THE CEREBRUM.

31

changed. Gage's misfortune showed that the brain has different parts, and spurred many scientists on to do more research.

Brain connections

You'll be pleased to know that your brain is so powerful and complex that it leaves computers behind. Why? Well, inside the brain there are about

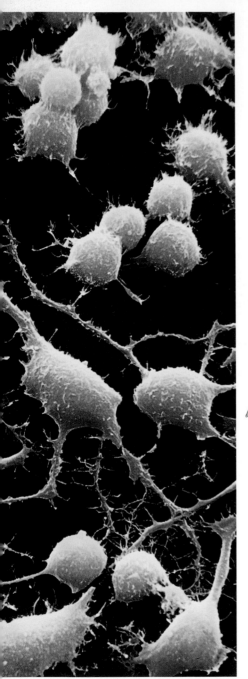

100 billion nerve cells, known as neurons. Neurons are slightly different from other body cells because they specialize in carrying electrical signals called nerve impulses at very high speed. Each one of these neurons has connections with hundreds or even thousands of

INSIDE YOUR BRAIN, NEURONS LIKE THESE PROCESS AND PASS ON IMPULSES AND INFORMATION AT LIGHTNING SPEED.

other neurons that together produce a massive communication network. This receives messages from sensors, for example, from inside the eye so you can see where you're going. It sends out instructions, so you can do things like walk in a straight line and digest your lunch. And the network analyzes and stores information so you think and remember.

between neurons. So people can be really bright – or not – regardless of their brain size.

B rain waves

"Having a brain wave" is one way to say that you've had a brilliant idea. But your brain actually gives off brain waves

LOG ON...
www.soton.ac.uk/~jrc3/chudler/neurok.html

AWAKE BUT RESTING

ALERT AND CONCENTRATING

SLEEPING DEEPLY

BRAIN WAVES PRODUCED BY ELECTRICAL SIGNALS DURING DIFFERENT ACTIVITIES

I ntelligence

The connections between all those billions of brain cells are also responsible for your intelligence. You might think men are more intelligent than women, because an average man's brain weighs 3 lb (1.35 kg) and a woman's weighs 2.75 lb (1.25 kg). But they aren't – intelligence does not depend on brain size, but on the number of connections

all the time, day and night. These are produced by the billions of electrical signals that flash between your brain's neurons every second. Brain waves vary depending on whether you are resting, really concentrating, or sleeping at the back of the class.

Why do you need to spend one-third of your life asleep?

33

Scientists think sleep gives your brain time to sort out the previous day's experiences, and gives your body a chance to rest. Without sleep, you would soon become weak and ill.

Sleeping and waking are part of a natural 24-hour rhythm controlled by the brain. This natural clock explains why you feel pretty tired at 3 a.m. and – hopefully – bright and

and a part of the left cerebral hemisphere sends instructions to the vocal cords in your throat so that you make sounds.

But there are other ways of getting your feelings across. Gestures and body language – the way your body is positioned when you talk or listen to people – are both important. The look on your face can also reveal how you feel.

I magine that

> How dull life would be if you weren't able to think up new ideas for yourself. Writing a story,

THIS PART OF YOUR BRAIN TELLS YOUR VOCAL CORDS TO MAKE SOUNDS AND COMMUNICATE.

alert at 10 a.m. These rhythms are easily disturbed, for example, by a long-distance flight to a different time zone.

THIS PART RECEIVES AND INTERPRETS NERVE SIGNALS FROM YOUR EAR AS YOU LISTEN.

Making contact

When you are wide awake, your versatile brain lets you communicate with other human beings. The way most humans do this is by speaking a common language. You think about what you want to say,

painting a picture, working out some new dance steps, or just explaining something in a different way, all depend on your brain's ability to be imaginative and creative. Most conscious creative thoughts and ideas come from the right cerebral hemisphere, the half that also deals with appreciating music and art. But imagination can also involve unconscious thoughts. These come from deep inside the brain and are where your basic emotions such as

Memory bank

Where would you be without your memory? You wouldn't be able to remember where you took your last vacation, learn anything new, recognize your friends, or even say something understandable. So it's a good

YOUR BRAIN HOLDS BILLIONS OF MEMORIES, SOME FOR LIFE

happiness and sadness also arise. Imagination is just another part of your intelligence, which also includes being able to solve problems, learn, and remember.

thing that your brain can sort out the information it receives, store what it wants to keep, and

VINCENT VAN GOGH (1853–90) USED HIS IMAGINATION TO CREATE THIS PAINTING.

recall what it needs when it needs it. A very simple way to look at memory is to divide it into two parts. Working – or short-term – memory briefly stores what's happening to you right now, like reading this sentence. Selected information – such as a scary film or an unusual phrase – is passed on and stored in long-term memory. This can then be recalled days, months, or even years later. Memories may be triggered by sights or smells that are stored in different parts of the brain.

THE SPINAL CORD AND NERVES CONNECT THE BRAIN TO THE REST OF YOUR BODY.

SPINAL CORD

What nerve!

Your brain links to the rest of your body via the spinal cord and nerves. Finger-thick and squishy, the spinal cord runs through your backbone and relays messages to and from the brain. Nerves pop out of the spinal cord and then branch out to carry nerve impulses to and from all parts of your body.

But the spinal cord is more than just an extension of the brain. It's also responsible for spilt-second responses called reflexes that protect you from everyday hazards. Touch your finger on a cactus, and what happens? A nerve impulse zooms up to your spinal cord, and – without having to think about it – straight back to an arm muscle that immediately pulls your hand away.

L osing your head

For a long time, a regular method of execution was beheading. Ouch! But, could the brain survive if its blood supply from the heart was cut off, and spinal cord connection severed? You may think it's impossible to answer this, because a headless person would be dead and unable to comment. But one enterprising French doctor decided to find out. In 1905, Dr. Beaurieux looked on as the guillotine

A GRUESOME
BEHEADING

WEIRD WORLD

IS A HEADACHE A PAIN IN THE BRAIN? NO IT ISN'T. YOUR BRAIN DOESN'T HAVE ANY SENSORS OF ITS OWN, SO IT CAN'T ACTUALLY "FEEL" PAIN. HEADACHES ARE COMMONLY CAUSED BY TENSION IN HEAD MUSCLES AND MEMBRANES SURROUNDING THE BRAIN.

sliced off the head of the notorious murderer Languille. When, seconds later, Beaurieux shouted "Languille!" at the severed head something weird happened. Three times in 30 seconds, the murderer's eyelids opened and he fixed his focused eyes on the doctor's.

B rain for life

Languille's brain must have been working for him to hear the doctor's voice and open his eyelids. The rest of his body was completely lifeless. This shows that the brain can survive without the body for a few seconds, but your body just can't survive without your brain.

BLOOD SUPPLY

E veryone knows what blood looks like, but do you know what it does? Bodies are made of trillions of cells, and each one demands a nonstop supply of food and oxygen. In order to provide this service, the heart pumps blood around the body – through blood vessels – in the circulatory system.

Crimson liquid

Thick, red, and runny, blood consists of billions of cells floating in a liquid called plasma. Most of these cells are the red blood cells that give blood its color. The rest are either white blood cells that hunt down and kill invading germs before they cause trouble, or platelets that offer a 24-hour repair service. If you cut yourself and damage a blood vessel, for example, the platelets stick together and plug the leak. Then you'd see a scab form over the plug to help the cut heal.

Supply service

Blood works like a delivery service – supplying oxygen, food, and other goodies to the body's cells, and removing waste like carbon dioxide, before it poisons the whole body. Blood also spreads heat around, so that

PLATELET

your body parts stay nice and warm at about 98.6°F (37°C).

Blood cells are carried around by plasma. This is mainly water but has more than a hundred different chemicals dissolved in it, including different types of food. One really important job – delivering oxygen – is the responsibility of the red blood cells. These dimpled deliverers are packed with an orangey-red substance called hemoglobin. As red cells whizz through the lungs, their hemoglobin loads up with the oxygen that has been breathed in. Then, when blood arrives in the big toe, earlobe, and every other part of the body that needs oxygen, the hemoglobin unloads its oxygen to satisfy demands.

BLOOD CONSISTS OF RED BLOOD CELLS, WHITE BLOOD CELLS, AND PLATELETS.

WEIRD WORLD

REGULAR BLEEDING WITH BLOOD-SUCKING LEECHES WAS ONCE A COMMON CURE FOR ILLNESS. LEECH "SALIVA" CONTAINS ANTI-CLOT CHEMICALS SO BLOOD FLOWS EASILY.

Pumping heart

To do its job, blood needs to be pumped around the body. This is the task of the heart. People once thought that the heart gave us our personality and feelings. We now know it is the brain that does that.

Used-up, or oxygen-poor, blood enters the heart from large veins. It goes first into the right atrium, which squeezes it into the right ventricle, and then onto the lungs to be refreshed with oxygen. It returns to the left side of the heart, through the left atrium, and into the left ventricle. The heart then pumps oxygen-rich blood to where it is needed – that is, everywhere in the body.

A CROSS-SECTION OF THE HEART

VALVES SLAM SHUT TO STOP BLOOD FROM GOING IN THE WRONG DIRECTION.

LEFT ATRIUM

THE LEFT VENTRICLE PUMPS OXYGEN-RICH BLOOD ALL AROUND THE BODY.

RIGHT ATRIUM

THE RIGHT VENTRICLE PUMPS OXYGEN-POOR BLOOD TO THE LUNGS TO BE RE-OXYGENATED.

Heartbeat

As you sit and read this, your heart is probably beating about 70 times each minute. A built-in pacemaker keeps it beating at the right rate. If you a car crash and used it to replace the heart of a man in his 50s who was dying from heart disease. Sadly, the man lived for just 18 days, but Dr. Barnard had showed that a

HEART MUSCLE NEVER TIRES AND NEVER TAKES A BREAK

exercise, the rate speeds up to make sure your muscles get more blood. During each heartbeat, both sides of your heart relax to draw in blood and then contract to squeeze blood either to the lungs or the rest of the body. With each beat, flappy heart valves close to stop blood from going in the wrong direction and make the thumping sounds you hear if you listen to someone's chest.

New hearts

Sometimes hearts don't work as well as they should and need replacing. Today, heart transplants are quite routine and can give people with serious heart disease a new lease on life. This operation was first pioneered in 1967 by South African surgeon Christiaan Barnard. He took the heart from a young woman who had just died in

heart transplant was possible.

Giving blood

A heart is not the only thing that can be moved from one body to another. We know how vital blood is – if a person loses too much, they die. The

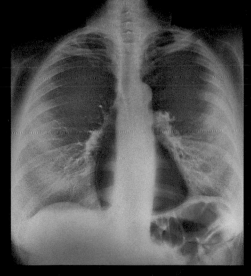

THE HEART (RED) SITS INSIDE YOUR CHEST, PROTECTED BY THE STERNUM AND RIBS.

idea of replacing lost blood by transfusion – taking blood from a donor (giver) and transfering it into a patient – was first considered in the 17th century. Attempts were made with blood from sheep, dogs, and then – sensibly – other humans. Some transfusions succeeded, but others made patients very ill or just killed them.

No one was really sure what was going on until Austrian doctor Karl Landsteiner (1868–1943) showed that there are four different types of blood. He called them A, B, AB, and O. Landsteiner also showed that if you gave the wrong type of blood to someone – for example if you gave a person with type A blood a transfusion of type B blood – their red blood cells would stick together. If this happened, small blood vessels could become blocked and the

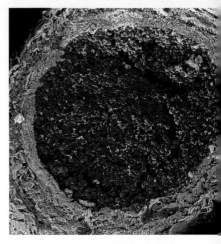

CROSS-SECTION OF A BLOOD-FILLED ARTERY

patient would die. Thanks to Landsteiner's discoveries, millions of safe blood transfusions now take place every day.

Tube transportation

It's great having a pump and the right kind of blood, but how does blood get everywhere it is needed? Fortunately, a massive tubular

MODEL SHOWS THE ARTERIES (RED) THAT DELIVER, AND VEINS (BLUE) THAT REMOVE, BLOOD FROM THE ARMS AND HANDS.

LOG ON...
www.bbc.co.uk/
science/humanbody/

network of blood vessels carries blood on the round trip to every nook and cranny of the body, and then back to the heart.

With each heartbeat, arteries carry blood away from the heart under high pressure. Luckily, artery walls are both strong and elastic. With each surge, the walls bulge outward and then spring back. You can feel this bouncing action where an artery comes near the surface of the skin, especially if it passes over a bone, like it does in your wrist just below the thumb. Each surge or pulse represents one heartbeat. Can you find your pulse? By keeping a finger on it, you can measure your heart rate.

Arteries branch all over the body, eventually leading into microscopic vessels called capillaries. These capillaries are so small that red blood cells sometimes have to bend sideways to fit inside them. Capillaries pass right by cells so that food and oxygen can pass from the blood and into the cells.

Back to your heart

Having done their job, the capillaries link up to form veins that carry oxygen-poor blood back to the heart. Veins have thinner walls, and the blood travels through them with only a small amount of pressure. Valves stop blood from flowing backward. Veins take blood back to the heart to begin another trip around the circulatory system.

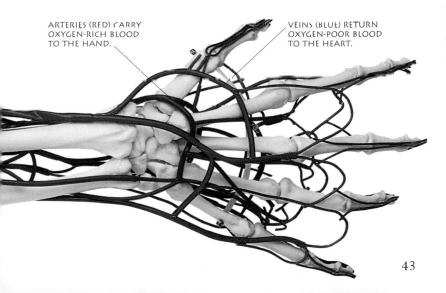

ARTERIES (RED) CARRY
OXYGEN-RICH BLOOD
TO THE HAND.

VEINS (BLUE) RETURN
OXYGEN-POOR BLOOD
TO THE HEART.

FOOD PROCESSOR

Y ou probably eat meals about three times a day. What happens between the food going into your mouth and waste coming out the other end? The answer is digestion. As food travels along your tubular intestines, it is broken down and digested to release all the nutrients you need to keep you alive and healthy.

N ecessary nutrients

What have you had to eat today? Some deep-fried grasshoppers or a few juicy caterpillars in tomato sauce? You might turn your nose up at these food items, but they are firm favorites in some parts of the world. What's more, they are as packed with nutrients as pizza and salad.

What are these vital nutrients? Carbohydrates and fats give you energy. Proteins help you grow and carry out body repairs. Vitamins, such as vitamin C, and minerals, such as iron, keep your cells working smoothly and you healthy. Fiber from fruits and vegetables gives your intestines a workout to keep them

GRASSHOPPERS CAN MAKE
A HEALTHY MEAL.

digesting properly. And last, but not least, water keeps you wet inside – among other jobs – and stops you from drying up like a wrinkled prune.

E nergy from food

Running, talking, even sitting still, are all activities that need energy. That energy comes from food, especially sugars and other carbohydrates.

How much energy you need depends on your age, sex, and what you do. A female athlete, for example, will need more energy than a woman who sits in an office all day. If you use the same amount of energy that you eat, your weight stays the same. People who eat more than they need store the extra energy as fat and get heavier.

NUTRIENTS ARE RELEASED FROM FOOD
WHILE IT IS IN THE DIGESTIVE SYSTEM.
THIS INCLUDES THE STOMACH (BLUE)
AND THE SMALL INTESTINE (GREEN).

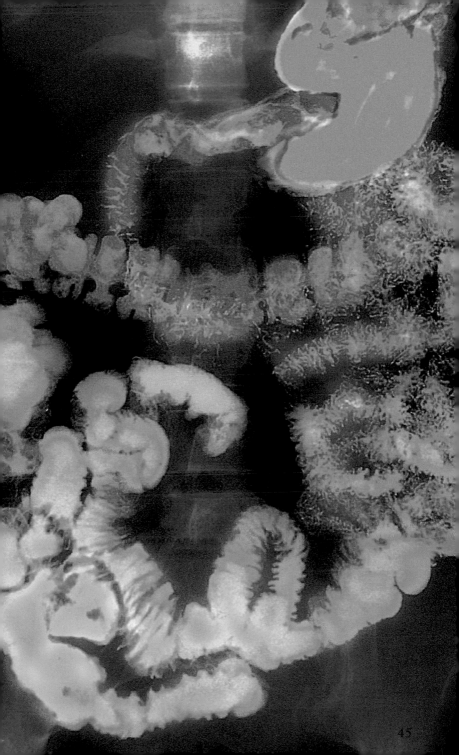

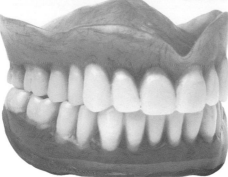

THESE FALSE TEETH SHOW INCISORS, CANINES, PREMOLARS, AND MOLARS.

carefully and you'll see the whole chewing process in living color!

Slippery swallow

Everywhere in the digestive system, thick, slimy mucus makes it easy for food to slip along the tubes. Mucus is certainly important when it comes to swallowing. Once food has been chewed into a ball, your tongue pushes it backward. The second it hits the throat, it is automatically pushed down a tube called the esophagus. Here a wave of muscle

Many teeth

The first stage of digestion is to get food inside your body. Unlike pythons, humans can't swallow their food in one big

BORBORYGMI IS THE SOUND-ALIKE NAME FOR DIGESTIVE NOISES

lump. Instead, we use our toothy tool kit to chop up food into pieces small enough to be swallowed. Incisor and canine teeth at the front of your mouth grab and cut up food. Big, flat premolars and molars at the back crush and grind. While the jaws are chomping, salivary glands squirt juicy saliva into the mixture, and your tongue mixes it all up. Usually your lips close to stop the food from falling out but, if you have a friend who eats with their mouth open, look

contractions squeezes food down to your stomach, in the same way that you'd squeeze a tube of toothpaste. The whole thing takes just 10 seconds.

Crush to a mush

Imagine taking your favorite meal, putting it into a blender, and whizzing it into a mush. That soupy slop is just what your meal would look like after it had been crushed and churned by your stomach. Chewed-up food arrives from the esophagus and is showered with acidic stomach juice that partly digests it and kills off most nasty bacteria. It is also pulverized by the crushing contractions of the stomach's muscular wall.

After about three hours in the stomach storage bag – longer if you've eaten greasy, fatty foods like double bacon cheeseburgers – food is gloopy enough to move on to the next phase of digestion. Every so often, the ring of muscle guarding the exit relaxes to let stomach soup squirt into the next section of your digestive system, the small intestine. But, if your stomach

TEETH AND TONGUE INSIDE THE MOUTH

MAIN PARTS OF THE DIGESTIVE SYSTEM

ESOPHAGUS

STOMACH

LARGE INTESTINE

SMALL INTESTINE

rejects what you've eaten, it might make you throw up by propelling the liquid food back up your esophagus and out of your mouth. Try not to be sick all over your bike, because the stomach acid in vomit will strip the paint off!

WILLIAM BEAUMONT EXPERIMENTING ON ALEXIS ST. MARTIN'S STOMACH.

Inside the stomach

Thanks to a gruesome accident, US surgeon William Beaumont pioneered understanding of how stomachs work. In 1822, he treated seriously wounded Alexis St. Martin who had accidentally shot himself in the side. St. Martin survived, but was left with a bullet hole into his stomach. For years – even when St. Martin objected – Beaumont carried out experiments on St. Martin's stomach, including dangling different types of food through the hole to see if they would digest. Beaumont's holey observations made him famous.

VILLI INSIDE YOUR SMALL INTESTINE SOAK UP FOOD AND TAKE IT TO YOUR BLOOD.

Small intestine

It seems a little odd to call the small intestine "small" when it's the longest part of your digestive system – it's called "small" because it's much narrower than the large intestine. Fortunately, it's all coiled up inside the abdomen. If it weren't, you would have to be a towering 21.3 ft (6.5 m) tall to fit it in.

When soupy food arrives from the stomach it is bombarded with digestive juices again. These juices contain lots of chemical digesters called enzymes that break food down into small useful bits like glucose and amino acids. Digested nutrients swirl around tiny villi, the mini-fingers that cover the inside of the small intestine. These vital villi soak up all the digested food and transfer it into the blood ready for speedy distribution to body cells.

Parasites

At one time, due to poor hygiene, it was common for parasites like enormously long, ribbonlike tapeworms to live in people's intestines. These uninvited guests wallow in the soupy food inside the small intestine and simply soak it up.

WEIRD WORLD
MONSIEUR MANGETOUT, A METAL-EATING FRENCHMAN, HAS EATEN MEALS OF BEER CANS, BICYCLES, AND SUPERMARKET CARTS. BUT HIS BIGGEST MEAL EVER WAS A CESSNA 150 LIGHT AIRCRAFT.

THE SUCKERS ON THE "HEAD" OF THIS TAPEWORM ALLOW IT TO CLING TO YOUR INTESTINES.

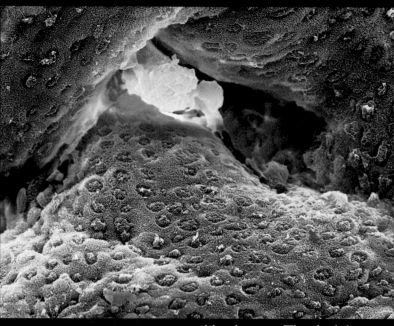

THE LARGE INTESTINE ABSORBS WATER
FROM ANY UNDIGESTED FOOD.

Hooks and suckers help
tapeworms latch onto the small
intestine wall so they aren't
swept away. Luckily, better
public health and cleanliness
has meant that few people get
worms from food these days.

Fecal factory

Feces, the brown stuff that
comes out when you defecate,
or go to the bathroom, are
made in the large intestine.
When a liquid delivery of
undigested food arrives in your
large intestine it really changes.
It dries out, as much-needed
water is returned back to the

bloodstream. The thick layer
of "friendly" bacteria lining the
large intestine breaks down any
food remnants to release the
gases that make farts, as well
as substances like skatole and
indole that give feces their
smell, and the brown stuff that
– well – gives feces their color.
Between 24 and 48 hours after
you swallowed that meal,
squishy feces arrive in the
rectum at the end of the large
intestine. A message from here
to the brain tells you that it's
time to visit the bathroom.

Upset tummy

While feces are supposed to be
nice and chunky, sometimes
they are watery and runny.

Having diarrhea can be a bit embarrassing because it often makes you need to go to the bathroom immediately. Diarrhea usually happens because you have eaten or drunk something contaminated with nasty bacteria. The body likes to get rid of it as quickly as possible.

Typhoid Mary

Getting diarrhea was a strong possibility if you ate food cooked by

Mary Mallon – a New York chef in the early 1900's. Everyone loved her cooking. What they didn't know was that she carried and passed on a nasty disease called typhoid. As well as causing really bad diarrhea, typhoid can kill.

As her employers and their families fell ill or died, Mary just moved from

job to job. Finally, in 1915, Mary was arrested and locked away for the rest of her life. Typhoid Mary's reign of terror and tummy trouble was over.

There is always a risk that food

_____

THE DIARRHEA-CAUSING BACTERIUM SALMONELLA TYPHIMURIUM

or drink may contain nasty bacteria, such as salmonella. These bugs use the digestive system as a way of getting inside your body. But despite the risk, we have to eat, drink, and digest to survive.

DEEP BREATH

Take a long, deep breath. Easy isn't it? Most people breathe in and out without thinking. When you breathe, oxygen races into your body and extracts energy from food, giving your cells power to do their important job. Taking in oxygen is the main role of the respiratory system, and without it we would die.

Oxygen supplies

Earth's atmosphere contains the gas – oxygen – which we need to stay alive. We automatically breathe in air containing oxygen through our mouth and nose – even when we're asleep.

This is all very well at ground level, but there are some places where there is not enough oxygen to support human life. For example, when mountaineers climb to high altitudes, the amount of oxygen decreases dramatically, and they need to breathe through masks connected to cannisters of oxygen. A similar situation applies to scuba divers.

Oxygen for energy

Wherever you are, at this very moment inside your cells tiny sausage-shaped mitochondria are using up oxygen. Why? To release energy stored in the glucose that you ate in recent meals. This energy powers the activities that keep your cells alive, and also keeps your insides warm. Carbon dioxide is produced as a waste.

Breathing in and out

For this important process to happen, your body has to

MITOCHONDRIA (GREEN) USE OXYGEN TO RELEASE ENERGY FROM FOOD.

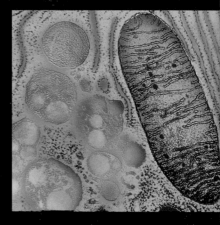

breathe air into your left and right lungs. They fill most of the space inside your chest. Breathing brings fresh supplies of oxygen into your lungs, and flushes out unwanted carbon dioxide. The body parts responsible for doing this are two sets of muscles – the diaphragm, a big sheet of muscle just below the lungs, and the rib muscles. When both contract, the ribs move up, the diaphragm down, and the space inside the chest increases, sucking air into the lungs. When the muscles relax and the space reduces, air is squeezed out of the lungs and you breathe out.

S oft lungs
Lungs are not hard and solid, as you might expect,

MAIN PARTS OF THE
RESPIRATORY SYSTEM

NASAL CAVITY

EPIGLOTTIS

LARYNX

TRACHEA

BRONCHIOLES

LUNG

DIAPHRAGM

53

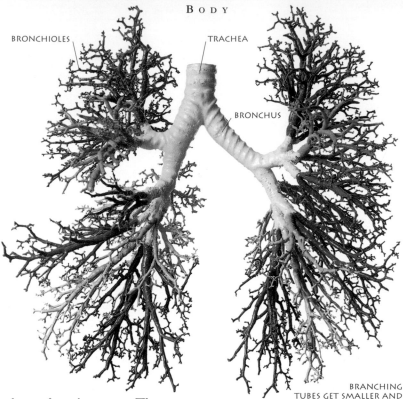

BRONCHIOLES

TRACHEA

BRONCHUS

BRANCHING
TUBES GET SMALLER AND
SMALLER INSIDE YOUR LUNGS

but soft and spongy. They are packed with masses of tubes that branch out from the bronchus, carrying air into each lung. The tiniest tubes inside your lungs – called bronchioles – end in microscopic air bags.

The name given to these air bags – and, no, it's not a type of pasta – is alveoli. Oxygen passes through the alveoli's paper-thin walls before being whisked away by the blood to the body's cells. In exchange, carbon dioxide goes in the opposite direction from the blood to the air inside your

alveoli. Then you breathe it out. Gas exchange is no small-scale operation. It's happening right now in the 300 million alveoli inside your lungs.

B reath control

As with most body parts, the brain is the control center. Your brain stem – where the brain joins the spinal cord – keeps you breathing in and out between 12 and 18 times a minute when you aren't doing much. If you start running, you breathe faster and deeper to get more oxygen into your body to release extra energy.

What a yawn!

Sometimes you may feel tired and yawn. No one's quite sure why one yawning person in a

nose has a built-in filter system. The sticky mucus layer inside traps particles. If you've ever spent time in a dusty room and then blown your nose, you'd see the stuff your nose has filtered from the air.

SPREAD OUT, ALVEOLI WOULD COVER ONE THIRD OF A TENNIS COURT

room sets off everyone else. But we think we know why you yawn. If you are bored or tired, your breathing slows down, and the level of carbon dioxide inside you increases. This triggers a really deep, open-mouthed breath – hand over mouth, please! – that flushes carbon dioxide out of the lungs and gets lots of fresh oxygen in. Unfortunately, if it's a really boring lesson, even a good yawn may not stop you from nodding off.

Trapping dirt

All that breathed-in air carries dust, dirt, and germs like bacteria and viruses. Any of these could damage delicate bronchioles or alveoli, so your

No smoking

The nose filter is not much help when it comes to cigarettes, because people smoke with their mouth. Smoke particles go directly to the lungs where they irritate tubes and air bags, and may cause lung cancer. Gases in

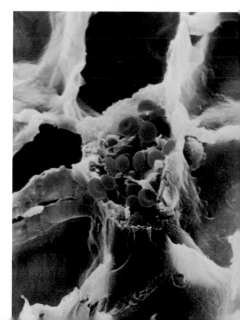

CROSS-SECTION OF ALVEOLI AROUND A BLOOD VESSEL. RED BLOOD CELLS INSIDE THE VESSEL COLLECT AND DISTRIBUTE OXYGEN.

cigarette smoke lower the amount of oxygen carried by red blood cells so smokers get breathless easily. And nicotine in cigarettes makes bronchioles narrower, so less air gets in and out of the lungs. These are good reasons not to smoke!

Stethoscope

Doctors can find out what's wrong with someone's breathing by listening with a stethoscope. It was French doctor René Laennec (1781–1826) who first came up with the idea. In Laennec's day, doctors had to put their ear right next to the patient's chest to hear them breathing. This could be embarrassing, and also a bit smelly if the patient hadn't washed! Laennec found that

A MODERN STETHOSCOPE

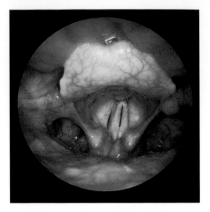

AIR RUSHING THROUGH CLOSED VOCAL CORDS MAKES THE SOUNDS OF SPEECH.

listening to the chest through a wooden tube not only avoided these problems but also made the sounds clearer. Laennec's wooden-tube stethoscope remained popular until 1852, when the modern version was invented.

Making sounds

One part of the respiratory – breathing – system lets you speak or sing. You can feel the larynx, or voice box, at the front of your neck – it's the bumpy part. Speak and you'll feel it vibrate. Stretched across it are two vocal cords. If they close, air rushing up from the lungs makes them vibrate and produce sounds. Your tongue and lips turn sounds into understandable words.

WEIRD WORLD

THE WORLD RECORD FOR HICCUPS IS HELD BY AN ENGLISH WOMAN WHO HICCUPED NONSTOP FOR 2 YEARS, 35 WEEKS, AND 3 DAYS DURING THE 1980'S. IN THE FIRST YEAR ALONE, SHE HICCUPED ONE MILLION TIMES.

Keep your tongue still and try to speak. It doesn't work very well, does it?

Choking and hiccups

Speaking and eating don't go very well together and can make you choke. A flap called the epiglottis normally folds over the larynx when you swallow to stop food from blocking your windpipe. But sometimes things go wrong, especially if you eat quickly and talk a lot. Unable to breathe, you start to choke. If this happens you automatically cough, clearing the blockage. A slap on the back may help too!

Eating too quickly can also trigger hiccups. A sudden contraction of the diaphragm sucks air into the lungs and makes the vocal cords smack shut to produce a loud "hic" noise. Normally hiccups don't last very long, especially if you hold your breath.

Explosive sneeze

Everyone gets a nose irritation from time to time. Dust or cold irritants trigger an automatic reflex action – the sneeze – that rapidly clears the nose. Sneezes happen like this. You take a deeper-than-normal breath, then send an explosive blast of air up through your nose. Droplets of watery mucus burst outward through your nostrils at speeds that can reach 100 mph (160 kmh). Pretty messy for the person standing in front of you! This is just one way your body keeps your respiratory system healthy.

THIS SPECIAL PHOTOGRAPH SHOWS THE AIR MOVED BY A SNEEZE.

BALANCING ACT

Your body's cells work best when the conditions around them are perfectly balanced. Never too hot or too cold, just enough water, and the right amount of food and oxygen. Helping to maintain this balance is the job of the urinary system, as well as the body's temperature regulators, and your hormones.

Urine makers

Making urine is the job of your two kidneys. Day and night they filter the blood to remove any excess water you might have drunk or eaten so that your blood doesn't get too diluted. They also remove unwanted waste, particularly stuff called urea that is made in the liver – a big organ that sits in your upper abdomen, near your stomach. It has about 500 different functions, mainly concerned with processing blood to make sure it contains the right ingredients.

The urine that you get rid of several times a day is made up of water and waste. How much urine you release varies from day to day. So if it's very hot and you sweat a lot, you make less urine. If it's cold and you have lots to drink, you make more.

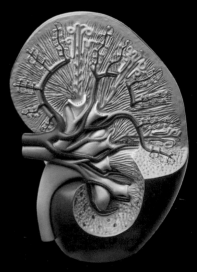

SECTION THROUGH A KIDNEY

Full to bursting

Three cheers for the bladder. Without it you would spend all day sitting on the toilet. Why? Because your kidneys produce a constant trickle of urine that runs into tubes called the ureters. Fortunately, instead of

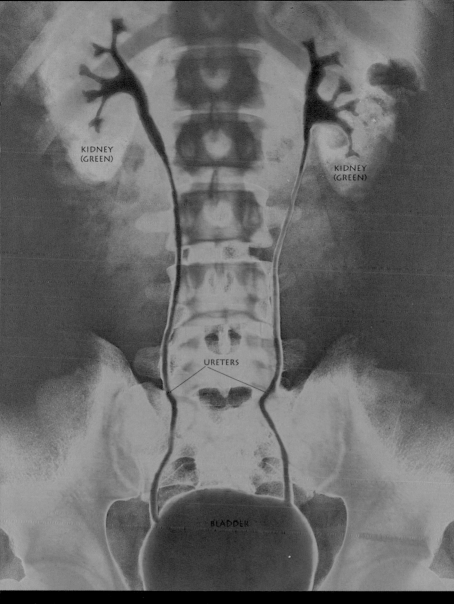

KIDNEY
(GREEN)

KIDNEY
(GREEN)

URETERS

BLADDER

releasing a nonstop stream to the outside of the body, the ureters empty into the bladder. At the base of this storage bag is an opening to the outside, normally kept closed by a ring of muscle called a sphincter. As

KIDNEYS (GREEN) MAKE URINE THAT TRICKLES DOWN THE URETERS TO THE BLADDER (ORANGE).

the bladder fills with urine, its muscular walls stretch and send messages to your brain. You gradually become aware that your bladder will soon need emptying. If you put it off, the feeling gets stronger and stronger until... you can delay it no longer, get to the toilet, and relax that sphincter muscle.

Urine test
Be thankful that you weren't a doctor in medieval times. Examining urine was one of the most important ways they had of finding out what was wrong with their patients. That meant not only looking at the color of the urine sample, sniffing it, and seeing if it was cloudy, but also – yuk! – tasting it. Modern doctors still do urine tests to help make a diagnosis, but luckily they are no longer required to taste it.

GOOSE BUMPS OCCUR WHEN YOU'RE COLD. YOUR HAIRS LIFT UP TO TRAP BODY HEAT.

drank (input), and his feces and urine (output), and himself. Sanctorio noted input was always greater than output, and suggested the difference was due to "insensible vapors." We know now that it was

YOUR BODY IS MADE UP OF ABOUT 60 PERCENT WATER

Sanctorio's input and output
One man who certainly had urine and balance on his mind was the Italian medical professor Sanctorius Sanctorio (1561–1636). For an amazing 30 years of his life – awake and asleep – Sanctorio spent as much time as possible sitting on a special weighing machine called "The Ballance." Daily he weighed whatever he ate and

caused mainly by water loss during sweating.

Temperature control
Sweating is part of the body's temperature control system. Chemical reactions going on inside your body cells constantly churn out heat. The layer of fat under your skin – and your clothes – also help to keep you warm.

When it's really cold, you probably get little bumps all over your skin – called goose bumps. You may also shiver. By suddenly contracting in a shivering shudder, your muscles release extra heat inside your body, and help to warm you up.

On the other hand, if it's very hot, blood vessels in your skin widen to make them give off heat more quickly, like a radiator. Sweat glands pour lots of watery, salty sweat onto your skin's surface. This evaporates – turns into water vapor – by sucking heat from the skin, so the body cools down. All these things help keep your body at a constant temperature of 98.6°F (37°C).

Water loss
Sweating is not the only way you lose water from your body. Every time you go to the bathroom you release water in urine and/or feces. When you breathe out, tiny droplets of water vapor escape from your mouth and nose.

But, more than half your body is water, and it needs to stay at that constant level. You can't afford to lose water without replacing it. Luckily, part of your brain called the thirst center realizes when your blood's getting too concentrated and tells you to have a drink. Drinking liquids replaces most of the 1.7–3.5 pints (1–2 liters) of water you lose each day. But you also get water from food, and not just squishy things like melons or cucumbers.

Hormones
Another part of the body's balancing act is played by hormones. These are chemicals

LOG ON...
www.yucky.kids.
discovery.com/body

BREATHING ON A MIRROR SHOWS THE WATER VAPOR YOU BREATHE OUT.

that make you become a boy or girl, grow, help you avoid danger, give birth (females only), and keep lots of other life functions in balance. Often called chemical messengers, most hormones are carried by the blood to particular target areas of the body where they have their effect.

They're mostly made by glands – a general name for body parts that make chemicals – called endocrine glands. Hormone headquarters are found in the pea-sized pituitary gland which hangs from the bottom of the brain. This releases lots of hormones that either have an immediate effect, or that tell other hormone-making glands what to do.

YOUR PITUITARY GLAND (GREEN) IS THE HORMONE HEADQUARTERS OF YOUR BODY.

Sugar levels

Hormones have very important jobs. One of these jobs is linked to glucose, which none

of us can do without. Glucose is the fuel we get from food that gives us the energy to stay alive. For that reason it's important to keep a constant level of glucose circulating in the blood. Regardless of whether you're starving hungry or have just eaten, every cell needs to have a nonstop supply.

Making sure that glucose is constantly on tap is the job of insulin and glucagon, two hormones released by the pancreas (just under your stomach). Glucagon increases blood glucose levels, while insulin brings them down, so

WEIRD WORLD

HUMANS ARE THE ONLY ANIMALS TO WEAR CLOTHES. BY HELPING TO MAINTAIN A STEADY BODY TEMPERATURE, CLOTHES HAVE ENABLED PEOPLE TO LIVE JUST ABOUT EVERYWHERE ON EARTH, EVEN THE ICY ARCTIC.

between them they keep the levels correct.

F ight or flight

Pounding heart, deep breathing, butterflies in the stomach, clammy hands, and shaky knees. Recognize the feeling? People experience it when they are alarmed or frightened by something. It's set off by the hormone adrenalin, which prepares the body for stress or

THE DANGERS OF EXTREME SPORTS SUCH AS ROCK CLIMBING CAN CAUSE AN ADRENALIN RUSH.

danger. If the brain thinks the body is threatened – whether its the sight of a charging bull, or climbing a sheer rock face high above the ground – it sends an express message to the adrenal glands. These sit on top of your kidneys and, when told to by the brain, release adrenalin into the bloodstream. Unlike most other hormones, adrenalin's effects are quick and short-lived. By speeding up heart rate and breathing, it gets more food and oxygen to your muscles. That way, you are ready to fight your way out of danger or run away as quickly as possible.

SKIN DEEP

Without skin you would look very red and gory. So it's a good thing we can't strip off this living overcoat to show off our glistening muscles underneath. Skin, along with hair and nails, marks the boundary between your insides and the outside world, and much more. It keeps out germs and water, filters the sun's rays, and lets you feel textures and surfaces.

Life on the surface
Look closely at the surface of the skin – a microscope helps – and the first thing you notice is that it's bumpy not flat, and has many nooks and crannies. These are packed with lots of bacteria. Most are harmless,

THIS MICROSCOPIC CROSS-SECTION VIEW OF THE SKIN SHOWS THE EPIDERMIS (PINK) AND DERMIS (YELLOW) LAYERS.

SURFACE CELLS KEEP SKIN WATERPROOF AND STOP GERMS FROM GETTING IN.

CELLS IN THE LOWER EPIDERMIS REPLACE SURFACE CELLS AS THEY ARE WORN AWAY.

DERMIS CONTAINS SWEAT GLANDS, HAIR ROOTS, BLOOD VESSELS, AND NERVE ENDINGS.

64

and do a good job in stopping harmful bacteria – and fungi – from growing on your skin. But they don't stay harmless if they manage to get into the body through cuts or scratches. That's why doctors rub bug-killing antiseptic onto the skin before they give an injection or operate. This helps to prevent bacteria from getting in.

Two layers

Dig downward from the surface, and you'd find your skin is only about 0.08 in (2 mm) thick. That's about as thick as 12 pages of this book. In places with more wear and tear – like the soles of your feet – its usually double that. Your thin skin is made up of two layers. On top is the epidermis that waterproofs the skin and stops germs from getting in. Its dead, flat cells are constantly replaced from below as they get rubbed away as skin flakes.

Skin, as well as hair and nails, contains a protein called keratin. The dead cells in the surface layer of the skin's epidermis are packed with keratin. This makes them tough, flexible, water-repellent, and able to carry out their important role until they get worn away as skin flakes.

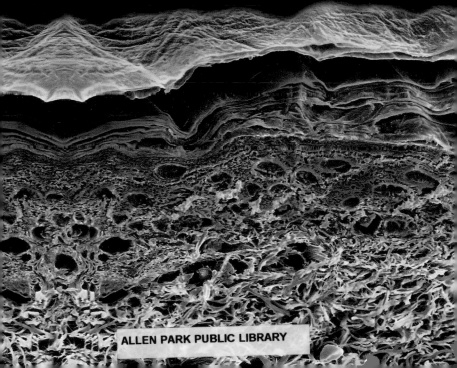

Hair and nails are both derived from the skin, so it's hardly surprising that they, too, are largely made of keratin. So flick a nail, run your fingers through your hair, or touch your skin, and you'll feel keratin at work in your body.

Under the epidermis is the thicker dermis. It contains blood vessels, sweat glands, your hair roots, and lots of nerve endings that let you sense pain, touch, heat, and cold.

Extra padding

Just under your dermis there's a layer of adipose tissue – or fat, as it's usually known. Fat acts as extra padding to protect your insides from

knocks and bangs, and works like a living comforter to help keep you warm. It also provides a backup energy store in the unlikely event that you run out of food. Some people eat more food than they need, and their under skin fat layer gets thicker and makes their skin stretch and bulge outward.

The big itch

One tiny animal that knows its way around the skin's layers is the itch mite, a microscopic relative of spiders. It's called the itch mite for one very good reason. It causes a disease called scabies that makes people itch so badly they just have to scratch and scratch until their skin bleeds. The male mite is

FAT CELLS ARE FOUND UNDER THE DERMIS.

harmless enough. The female, on the other hand, uses piercing mouthparts to dig a burrow through the epidermis into the dermis where she lays her eggs and causes the awful itching. Fortunately for those affected, scabies can be cured using mite-killing lotions.

Skin color

From the palest pink to the darkest brown, skin color varies enormously. What color your skin is depends on the amount of a pigment (coloring) called melanin. This brown-black pigment is made by cells in the epidermis. People with very dark skin produce lots of melanin while those with pale skin produce little melanin. Some people have little patches of skin with extra melanin, better known as freckles. The other thing that colors your skin is the pinkness produced by blood flowing through it. This is less obvious if you have dark skin than if it is pale.

Sun protection

The reason melanin is important is because it screens out harmful rays in sunlight called ultraviolet (UV) rays. That's why people who live in – or whose ancestors originally came from – hot places like

SUNSCREEN WILL PROTECT THESE PEOPLE FROM BURNING IN THE SUN'S UV RAYS AND THEIR SKIN WILL GRADUALLY DARKEN.

Ethiopia have darker skin. Their skin naturally produces more melanin for protection from the hot sun than pale-skinned people. Spend time in the sun, and your skin automatically makes extra protective melanin and gives you a suntan. Even so, too much time spent uncovered

WEIRD WORLD
BLEEDING FROM TINY BLOOD CAPILLARIES IN OR UNDER THE SKIN PRODUCES THE FAMILIAR BLACK-AND-BLUE MARK KNOWN AS A BRUISE. IN TIME, THE BRUISE TURNS YELLOW AND THEN EVENTUALLY FADES AWAY.

under a hot sun – especially if you're not coated with sunscreen – and the UV rays will burn your skin, causing the painful, hot redness of sunburn.

Overactive glands

Keeping your skin – and hair – soft and supple is the job of sebaceous glands. These glands release an oily liquid called sebum that lubricates your skin and helps keep it waterproof. That's the good news. Unfortunately, sometimes the tube from the gland gets blocked with sebum, causing pimples. If the sebum blockage darkens near the surface, you get a blackhead. Or, the blockage may encourage bacteria to get to work and make things red and infected, in which case you develop acne. Teenagers tend to get pimples because their hormones encourage the sebaceous glands to work harder.

WEIRD WORLD

VITAMINS ARE GENERALLY OBTAINED FROM FOOD, BUT ONE – VITAMIN D – IS ALSO MADE BY THE SKIN WHEN IT IS EXPOSED TO SUNLIGHT. VITAMIN D ENABLES THE BODY TO USE CALCIUM TO STRENGHTEN BONES AND TEETH.

Armpit odors

As if that weren't enough, you also start to sweat under the arms when you reach puberty. Coiled up in the dermis are the sweat glands that release cooling sweat onto the skin's surface when you are hot. The ones in the armpits release a slightly different sort of sweat. Armpit sweat doesn't smell until bacteria feed on it and release substances that are musky and smelly. That's what gives people who don't wash often, or who don't use deodorants, a strong smell of body odor.

Fingerprints

Even your fingertips sweat. Touch glass or metal, and you'll see fingerprints – sweat marks left by your fingers. The curves and loops of fingerprint patterns are produced by skin ridges that help you grip things when you pick them up. No two people have the same pattern of ridges, not even identical twins. At the end of the 19th century, someone realized that sweat patterns left at the scene of a crime could be used to identify criminals. Ever since then, fingerprinting has played an important part in crime detection.

Some criminals have tried to remove their fingerprints so that they couldn't be easily identified at crime scenes. The gangster John Dillinger got two doctors to remove his fingerprints with plastic surgery in 1934. It was a failure, so next he tried dipping his fingers in acid until the ridge patterns disappeared. Ouch! In the end even this didn't work. By the time he was caught by the FBI later that same year, Dillinger's fingerprints had reappeared and he was once again identifiable.

C urly and straight hair

Another distinguishing feature you have is your hair. It can vary in color, and you can cut, braid, bead, or even shave it off. Hairs grow from holes in the skin called follicles that are dotted around your body except for your soles, palms, lips and one or two other places. Whether you are naturally curly, wavy, or straight-haired depends on what shape your follicles are. A round follicle makes straight hair, oval makes wavy, and flat makes curly.

P ainless haircut

Hairs grow from the follicles as tubes of dead cells which consist mainly of keratin. That's why it doesn't hurt when you have

CLOSE-UP OF A MAN'S SHAVED FACIAL HAIRS

LOG ON...
www.brainpop.com/health/

your hair cut. Each head hair grows about 0.08 in (2 mm) a week for a few years before it is pushed out of the follicle by a new hair. Left uncut, hair can reach 3 ft (90 cm) long before it stops growing. In exceptional cases, some people have been able to grow hair up to 13 ft (4 m) long, which is OK unless someone steps on it!

Hair grippers

All that hair can attract unwanted attention from head lice – tiny blood-sucking insects. If disturbed while biting through the scalp, head lice move as quick as a flash, and grab ahold of the nearest hair with their "claws" so they don't get dislodged. What's more, female lice actually glue their eggs – called nits – to individual hairs so they don't get swept away when someone washes their hair. Head lice are common among school children, and they spread like wildfire from head to head. Special shampoos kill off the lice, while fine-toothed nit combs get rid of the eggs.

B ald facts

Some people are not as likely to get head lice because they are bald. For some men,

Nails, also made of keratin, are really useful when you have an itch to scratch, or when you are trying to pick up something small. They grow at about 0.2 in (5 mm)

CUTAWAY VIEW OF A FINGER, SHOWING BONES, LAYERS OF TISSUE, AND THE NAIL.

OF THE 100,000 HAIRS ON YOUR HEAD, 80 ARE REPLACED EVERY DAY

the hairs on top of their head grow for such a short time that the hair doesn't even have a chance to emerge above the surface of the skin before it is pushed out by the hair below.

N ails at work

Not everyone has a full head of hair, but everyone has nails.

every month – a little faster in summer than in winter. Most people cut their nails as they grow. But one man who didn't cut his nails grew them to over 3 ft 4 in (1 m) long. His thumbnail was the longest nail – it was 4 ft 7 in (1.4 m) long. He obviously didn't work as a painter or a dentist!

RUNNING REPAIRS

The human body is often referred to as a living machine; and like all machines, it can break down from time to time. If things do go wrong, the body can often repair itself, sometimes with the help of doctors. However, not all illnesses start inside the body. Some are triggered by invaders from outside.

Enemy invaders

Germs or bugs are always hanging around, trying to get inside your body. Those that succeed can make you ill.

are two main types of cells in your blood. Red cells carry oxygen, but white cells do something very different. At the first sign of invasion by

HARMLESS BACTERIA LIVE IN YOUR INTESTINES AND ON YOUR SKIN

These pathogens – the proper name for microscopic, disease-causing invaders – include viruses and bacteria. Unluckily for them, your body has a super-strong defense system, and without it you wouldn't last very long. Any pathogens that manage to get in face a deadly army of loyal defenders.

Eat and destroy

One of these defenders is your blood. There

pathogens, white cells called phagocytes rush to the site of infection, find the pathogens, and then gobble them up.

PATHOGEN

72

For any pathogens that survive that onslaught, the body has an even deadlier weapon.

This is the immune system, the most sophisticated part of your body's defenses. Playing a key role in the immune system are white blood cells called lymphocytes. These long-living cells keep a record of all the pathogens that have gotten into your body. If a pathogen

A PHAGOCYTE
(YELLOW)
ENGULFING A
PATHOGEN (GREEN)

shows up again, lymphocytes release a killer substance called an antibody which targets that pathogen and knocks it out.

Just the needle

It sounds like the body's defenses are very good. So why is it that some pathogens are much more dangerous than others? Why, for example, is meningitis so much more serious than the common cold? Well, some pathogens multiply very rapidly inside the body and cause serious illness before the immune system has had time to get its act together. Fortunately, modern medicine has found a way around this.

Doctors can stop people from getting a particular disease by injecting a vaccine into their body. A vaccine contains a weak or dead version of the pathogen. This makes the immune system produce antibodies but doesn't cause any illness. If the real pathogen then turns up, it gets wiped out by the army of antibodies that's already waiting there.

Discovering antibiotics

Antibiotics give doctors another weapon in the war against germs. They were discovered by chance in 1928 by Alexander Fleming in London. While studying bacteria, one of his experiments got contaminated with the blue-gray mold you find on rotting fruit. But what really surprised him was that the mold was killing the bacteria.

The bacteria-killing chemical was isolated from this mold and called penicillin. It was the first of many bacteria-killing drugs, or antibiotics, that have proved to be real lifesavers.

Blood clots

Invasion by pathogens is one thing, but what happens if

RED BLOOD CELLS CAUGHT IN A FIBRIN NET TO FROM A BLOOD CLOT.

internal body parts go wrong.
Like a hole in a blood vessel,
for example. Left unrepaired,
blood would just leak out. So
it's a good thing the body has
its own pipe repair service.
Whenever a blood vessel is
split or torn, tiny platelets
carried by the blood pile into
the damage zone and "stick" to
each other to plug the leak.

Platelets also do something
else. Sticky platelets release
chemicals that dissolve a blood
protein called fibrinogen into
fibers of fibrin. Just like a
fishing net, these fibers trap red
blood cells and other blood
pieces to form a clot that
reinforces the platelet plug.
While plug and clot stop the
leak, the blood vessel wall has
time to rebuild itself.

F ix that fracture

Another built-in repair system
fixes bones if they fracture
or break. Bones are really
strong. But sudden, extra
pressure from an
unusual angle – if
someone falls off
their bike, for
example – can make
a bone break. If
that happens,
bone healing

AN X-RAY OF BADLY
BROKEN ARM BONES.

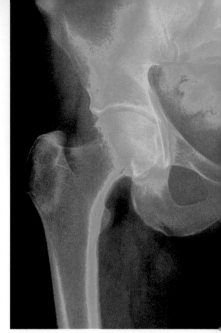

begins immediately. A clot forms to stop bleeding from the broken ends and new bone grows to join them together. With time, the bone looks as good as new. But fracture repair may need some medical help so the bones heal straight, not bent. To do this, bones may be set in a cast or have pins put in them.

S urgery

Sometimes, the skills of a surgeon are required to fix the body. These doctors operate on the body by cutting into it to make repairs. The person being operated on feels no pain because they are given an anesthetic that makes them unconscious for awhile. But this wasn't always the case.

Before 1846, when ether – an anesthetizing gas – was first used by American William Morton, operations, such as amputations, had to be carried

out as quickly as possible. Patients were either tied to the operating table or held down by strong men!

K eeping it clean

A surgeon called Joseph Lister (1827–1912) also improved the chance of surviving surgery. He recognized the importance of keeping clean, and introduced bug-killing chemicals called antiseptics to spray in and around wounds to kill germs. Later on, asepsis was introduced. This involved sterilizing surgical instruments to kill pathogens, cleaning the operating room with disinfectant, and wearing clean gowns and protective masks – just like surgery today.

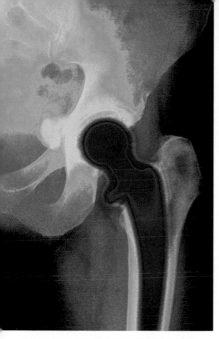

X-RAY SHOWS THE METAL PART (PINK) USED IN A HIP-REPLACEMENT OPERATION.

http://tqjunior.thinkquest.org/5777/

LOG ON...

replace diseased joints with artificial ones, or worn-out heart valves with metal and plastic replacements. More and more old body parts can be replaced by new ones when needed.

F it and healthy

In the end, though, you can't beat looking after your body properly so that it only requires the minimum of repairs. A fit body – one that works well – is more likely to be healthy and last longer. Unfortunately, compared to our ancient ancestors, who were forever chasing after antelopes or running away from lions, our modern lifestyle tends to involve much more sitting around, playing with computers, watching television, and eating junk food. So, to keep your body fit it needs daily exercise and a mixed diet that includes plenty of fruits and vegetables and not too much fat.

N ew body parts for old

Centuries ago, pirates and sailors who had legs or arms blown off in sea battles would replace the missing part with a wooden "peg leg." Things are a littler more advanced now. The latest replacement arms and legs are lifelike and lightweight. Surgeons can operate on the body to

PLAYING SPORTS HELPS KEEP YOUR BODY FIT AND HEALTHY.

LIFE STORY

We all follow the same life story. Have you ever heard of a person who has gotten younger, or anyone who is born at the age of 15? You might want to skip some parts of life, but you can't. We are all born as babies, grow slowly through childhood, change rapidly in our early teens to grow into adults, maybe have children ourselves, and then grow old gracefully.

Frankenstein

Changing the normal life story should be impossible, unless you have the fertile imagination of English author Mary Shelley. In 1818, she wrote a book about a scientist – Victor Frankenstein – who collected parts from dead bodies, and sewed them together to make a new "man." His creation was brought to life using the power of lightning. Frankenstein's monster had a fairly miserable life, and in the end he destroyed the man who had made him.

Race for the egg

In real life, adults who want to make a new human being do it the natural way – by having a baby – not by stitching body parts together. Two vital ingredients are needed –

SPERM CLUSTER AROUND AN EGG, BUT ONLY ONE WILL GET INSIDE TO FERTILIZE IT.

EGG

SPERM

one sperm from father and one egg from mother. While a woman releases just one egg each month from her ovaries, a man makes millions of sperm inside his testes. He releases these inside his partner when the couple become very intimate and make love. Most of the sperm fall by the wayside as they swim wildly toward the egg – if there is one – in the fallopian tube that runs

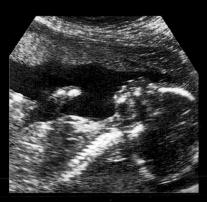

ULTRASOUND SHOWS A BABY GROWING INSIDE ITS MOTHER'S UTERUS.

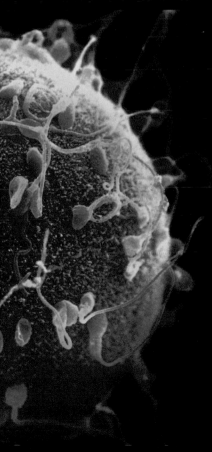

between the ovary and the uterus. Of the few sperm that reach the egg, one manages to get inside and fertilize it. A few days later, the fertilized egg has divided to form a ball of cells which sinks into the soft and warm uterus lining and starts to develop into a baby.

Growing inside
It's happened to all of us, although it's doubtful any of us can remember it. The event in question? Being born. Traveling from the warm, quiet, dark surroundings of our mother's uterus, we are thrust into the bright, noisy outside world with all those people making strange noises. Birth happens about 40 weeks after fertilization. In that short time, we have developed from the microscopic ball of cells that snuggled down in the lining of

the uterus, to a 6.5 lb (3 kg) baby with all organs up and running. This includes lungs for loud crying, and fully operative urinary and digestive systems for diaper filling.

It's all in the genes

When a new baby does arrive, it's not unusual for people to say how much she or he looks like her or his mother or father. Are they telling the truth, or not? They probably are. Every human being inherits two sets of body-building instructions, called genes – one from the mother's egg and one from the father's sperm. Genes interact to make us what we are, with some maternal features, some paternal features, and some that are unique to us as individuals. All these genes – and there are about 30,000 in each set – are strung along 46

"threads" called chromosomes found in every cell. Chromosomes – and genes – are made of a long molecule called DNA, or deoxyribonucleic acid. DNA molecules contain the instructions, in code, to build and operate each of the cells in your body – and to construct and complete a human being.

Double trouble

Humans usually only have one baby at a time. But not always. Sometimes women have two (twins), occasionally three (triplets), or, even more

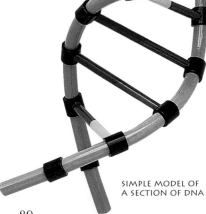

rarely, four (quadruplets). So, why do twins happen? Usually, one egg is released each month by one of a woman's two ovaries. But if, by chance, two eggs are released, and both are fertilized by different sperm, they will grow into twins. These twins are not identical because, being made by different eggs and sperms, they don't share the same genes.

SIMPLE MODEL OF A SECTION OF DNA

They could both be girls, both boys, or one of each. Identical twins do share the same genes. They happen when a fertilized egg splits into two separate cells, each of which grows into a baby. They have to be the same sex, and often look so similar that they manage to confuse everybody!

IDENTICAL TWINS ARE FORMED WHEN A FERTILIZED EGG SPLITS INTO TWO TO MAKE TWO BABIES.

L earning zone
Learning about things goes on throughout life, but the busiest time for it is during childhood. Just think of the things you have learned and are learning. How to crawl, walk, run, throw a ball, write, spell, speak, control when you want to go to the bathroom... the list is endless. Your brain soaks up information like a sponge, so that you can increase your word power or become better at using a computer. Other

WEIRD WORLD
IN 2000, THE HUMAN GENOME PROJECT IDENTIFIED THE STRUCTURE OF THE GENES INSIDE HUMAN CHROMOSOMES. THAT MEANS THEY'VE TAKEN THE FIRST STEP TO WORK OUT PLANS TO MAKE A HUMAN BEING.

things, like walking or riding a bike, you learn by trying and then using the experience to make improvements.

Growing pains

Once girls are between 9 and 13, and a little later in boys, big changes happen – puberty

children look like adults. It also changes the way they think and feel as well.

Old and wrinkly

If you didn't get older, you wouldn't have any birthdays, so life just wouldn't be as much fun. And while it's obvious that

ABOUT ONE IN EVERY 80 BIRTHS PRODUCES TWINS

has arrived. This is the time when both girls and boys have a sudden growth spurt, the first time they've grown so quickly since they were babies! Their body shapes change, so they look more like adults, and their reproductive systems "switch on" so they can – when they're ready – have babies.

In charge of these changes are sex hormones. Before you were born, these hormones sorted out whether you were going to be a boy or girl. Now, at puberty, they trigger your body changes.

Puberty is part of adolescence, the growing up process that makes

children grow into adults, you don't really notice signs of aging until people are in their 40s and 50s. It's around this time that the body's cells start

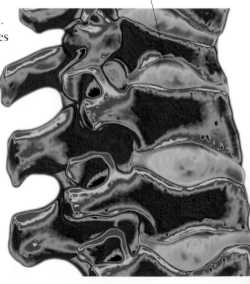

VERTEBRA THAT HAS BEGUN TO CRUMBLE.

THIS SCAN OF A BACKBONE SHOWS HOW ONE VERTEBRA HAS STARTED TO SHOW THE SIGNS OF AGING.

LOG ON...
www.genetics.about.com/science/genetics/cs/humangenome/index.htm

getting less efficient. On the outside, the skin gets less elastic and more wrinkly, and the hair gets thinner and can turn gray or white. On the inside, the eyes don't focus quite as well, muscles lose some of their strength, and bones become more brittle. In the end, one or other body system stops working, and the person dies.

However, it's worth remembering that, thanks to good public health and modern medicine, we live much longer than our ancestors did. Good food and plenty of exercise helps as well. Lots of people survive into their 90s and 100s, and – just occasionally – into their 120s.

Into the freezer

Death may be inevitable, but some people still try to avoid it. In recent years it's become possible to pay to have your body deep frozen around the time you die. And deep frozen means just that – a very chilly -321°F (-196°C). The hope is that a deep-frozen body can be defrosted at some time in the future, when doctors know how to cure the disease that killed it. Sounds good, but there are a couple of problems. First, there's no guarantee that the body can actually be woken up from its "frozen sleep." More importantly, would your descendants actually be bothered to unfreeze their ancestors?

A BODY BEING DEEP FROZEN

Well-preserved

Of course, the other way to continue on after death was to get yourself mummified. The mummy experts of the ancient world were the Egyptians. They believed that when you died, your soul left the body, but that they joined up again later. Without a body for the soul to return to, there was no chance of an afterlife. So, the Egyptians used their skills to preserve bodies, although in a rather dried-up form.

People have had their nearest and dearest mummified more recently as well. In Sicily, Italy, there are some 6,000 mummies dating from 1599 to 1920 in an underground cemetery. Wealthy Sicilians had their relatives mummified as a memento of what was once a living, breathing body.

But, however life ends, the path from fertilization to old age is full of change and growth. We each start as a ball of cells, become babies, then children, teenagers, and finally adults, before growing old. This is the body's life story.

RELATIVES CAN VISIT THEIR DEAD, WELL-PRESERVED, FAMILY MEMBERS IN THESE SICILIAN UNDERGROUND TOMBS.

REFERENCE SECTION

Whether you've finished reading *Body*, or are turning to this section first, you'll find the information on the next eight pages really helpful. Here are all the historical facts and figures, background details, body statistics, and unfamiliar words that you will need. You'll also find a list of website addresses – so, whether you want to surf the net or search for facts, these pages should turn you from an enthusiast into an expert.

BODY TIMELINE

c.100,000 BC Modern humans (Homo sapiens) first appear in Africa.

c.70,000 BC Humans spread from Africa to other continents.

c.30,000 BC Cave paintings and sculptures show the shape of the human body.

c.420 BC Greek physician Hippocrates teaches the importance of observation and diagnosis – rather than magic and myth – in medicine.

c.170 Influential Greek doctor Galen describes – often incorrectly – the workings of the body, and his ideas remain mostly unchallenged until the 1500s.

c.1000 Arab doctor Avicenna publishes medical texts that would influence Western medicine for the next 500 years.

c.1280 Arab doctor Ibn An-Nafis proposes that blood flows through the lungs.

1543 First accurate description of human anatomy published by Belgian anatomist Andreas Vesalius.

1628 British doctor William Harvey describes how blood circulates around the body, pumped by the heart.

1663 Italian physiologist Marcello Malpighi discovers blood capillaries.

1672 Dutch doctor Regnier de Graaf describes the structure and workings of the female reproductive system for the first time.

1674 Dutchman Antoni van Leeuwenhoek observes and describes red blood cells, sperm, and skeletal muscle cells using an early microscope.

1691 British doctor Clopton Havers describes the structure of bones.

1796 First vaccination – against smallpox – by British doctor Edward Jenner.

1811 British anatomist Charles Bell shows that nerves are made of bundles of neurons (nerve cells).

1816 French doctor René Laënnec invents the stethoscope.

1846 Ether gas first used as an anesthetic in surgery by US dentist William Morton.

1848 French scientist Claude Bernard demonstrates the function of the liver, and later shows that body cells need to live in stable surroundings.

1851 German physicist Hermann von Helmholtz invents the ophthalmoscope, an instrument for looking inside the eye.

1860s French scientist Louis Pasteur explains how microorganisms cause infectious diseases.

1865 Joseph Lister, a British doctor, first uses antiseptic during surgery to reduce deaths from infection.

1882 German doctor Robert Koch identifies bacterium that causes TB (tuberculosis).

1895 Wilhelm Roentgen, a German physicist, discovers X-rays.

1901 Austrian-born US doctor Karl Landsteiner discovers blood groups A, B, AB, and O, and paves the way for safe blood transfusions.

1903 An early version of the ECG (electrocardiograph), a device for monitoring heart activity, is invented by Dutch physiologist Willem Einthoven.

1906-12 British biochemist Frederick Gowland Hopkins shows importance of vitamins in food.

1910 German scientist Paul Ehrlich discovers the first drug used to treat a specific disease.

1921 Canadians Frederick Banting and Charles Best isolate the hormone insulin, enabling the disease diabetes to be controlled.

1928 British doctor Alexander Fleming discovers penicillin, the first antibiotic.

1943 Dutch doctor Willem Kolff invents the kidney dialysis machine to treat people with kidney failure.

1953 Using research by British physicist Rosalind Franklin, US biologist James Watson and British physicist Francis Crick discovers the structure of DNA.

1953 American surgeon John Gibbon develops the heart-lung machine to pump blood during heart surgery.

1954 First use of the polio vaccine developed by US doctor Jonas Salk.

1954 First successful kidney transplant carried out in Boston, Ma.

1958 First use of ultrasound to check fetus health inside a uterus by British professor Ian Donald.

1967 South African surgeon Christiaan Barnard carries out the first successful heart transplant.

1972 CT (computerized tomography) scanning used to produce images of body organs.

1978 Successful IVF (in vitro fertilization) by British doctors Patrick Steptoe and Robert Edwards results in first "test tube" baby, Louise Brown.

1979 Vaccination finally eradicates the disease smallpox from the world.

1980s Introduction of "keyhole" surgery – using an endoscope to look inside the body.

1981 The disease, later to be named AIDS (acquired immune deficiency syndrome), first identified.

1982 First artificial heart, invented by US scientist Robert Jarvik, is implanted into a patient.

1984 French scientist Luc Montagnier discovers the virus – later called HIV – that causes AIDS.

1990 Human Genome Project is launched to analyse the DNA in human chromosomes.

2000 First "draft" of the Human Genome Project is completed.

BODY SYSTEMS

SYSTEM	FUNCTION
Circulatory system	Pumps blood along a network of blood vessels to transport nutrients and oxygen to cells, and remove their wastes.
Digestive system	Breaks down food into simple nutrients that can be used by the body.
Endocrine system	Releases hormones (chemical messengers) into the blood which control several body processes.
Immune system	Defends the body against the bacteria and viruses that cause diseases.
Integumentary system	Consists of the skin, hair, and nails that cover and protect the body.
Lymphatic system	Drains fluid (lymph) from the tissues from which it filters out pathogens.
Muscular system	Moves and helps support your body.
Nervous system	Controls and coordinates the body, and enables a person to think and feel.
Respiratory system	Carries oxygen from the air into the blood, and removes waste carbon dioxide from the body.
Skeletal system	Supports the body, protects internal organs, and permits movement.
Reproductive system	Enables humans to produce children.
Urinary system	Removes waste materials and excess water from blood to be released as urine.

AMAZING FACTS

Cells
- 3 billion body cells die and are replaced every minute.
- Cells lining the small intestine are worn way after 3 to 6 days.
- Red blood cells are worn out by the time they are 120 days old.
- Liver cells live for about 18 months.

Skeleton and muscle
- An adult has 206 bones but a newborn baby has more than 300.
- The body's bulkiest muscle is the gluteus maximus in the buttocks.

Nervous system, brain, senses
- A nerve impulse takes just one-hundredth of a second to travel from big toe to spinal cord.
- Although the brain makes up just 2 percent of body weight, it receives 20 percent of the body's blood supply at all times, whether the body is at rest or exercising.

Circulatory system
- A drop of blood has 250 million red blood cells, 16 million platelets, and 375,000 white blood cells.
- The heart beats nearly 3 billion times in a lifetime without ever stopping to rest.
- Stretched out, one person's blood vessels would go around the Earth two and a half times.
- The biggest artery – the aorta – is 2,500 times wider than the smallest capillaries.

Digestion
- Tooth enamel contains no living cells. If it's damaged it cannot be replaced, except by a filling.
- In an average lifetime, a person eats 30 tons of food.
- On average, people release enough farts each day to fill a party balloon.

Breathing
- On average, a person breathes in and out about 25,000 times a day.
- The left lung is smaller than the right lung because it has to fit around the heart.

Urinary system
- Daily, the kidneys filter 40 gallons (180 liters) of fluid from blood but produce just 0.33 gallons (1.5 liters) of urine.
- In a lifetime, a person releases 7,870 gallons (35,770 liters) of urine.

Skin
- About 50,000 tiny flakes drop off the skin every minute.
- Fingernails grow four times faster than toenails.
- Itches are caused by irritating dust particles getting into hair follicles.

Body defenses
- The eyes blink on average about 9,400 times a day.
- Tears contain a chemical called lysozyme that kills bacteria on the surface of the eye.
- More than 10 billion white blood cells are produced daily to destroy invading pathogens.

Reproduction
- A man's two testes produce more than 300 million sperm every day.
- When girls are born, they already have more than a million eggs present in their ovaries.

BRANCHES OF MEDICINE

Anatomy The structure of the body and how its parts fit together

Biochemistry The chemicals in and around body cells, and how they react with each other

Cardiology The heart and blood vessels, and their diseases

Cytology The study of cells

Dermatology The skin and its diseases

Endocrinology Endocrine glands and their diseases, and the effects of hormones on the body

Epidemiology How diseases are caused and spread within and between groups of people

Gastroenterology The digestive system and diseases

Genetics Genes, chromosomes, and inheritance

Gynecology The female reproductive system and its diseases

Hematology The study of blood, and diseases affecting blood and bone marrow

Histology The study of tissues

Immunology The immune system and what goes wrong with it

Neurology The nervous system and its diseases

Obstetrics Pregnancy and childbirth

Oncology The causes and treatment of cancers

Ophthalmology The eye and its diseases

Orthopedics Bones, joints, muscles, tendons, and ligaments, and how they go wrong

Pediatrics The growth and development of children, and childhood diseases

Pathology The causes and effects of diseases, and the causes of death

Physiology How cells, tissues, organs, and systems work

Psychiatry Mental illness and its treatment

Radiology Use of X-rays and other imaging techniques to investigate and treat diseases

Urology Urinary system in males and females and its diseases, and the reproductive system in males

BODY WEBSITES

www.bbc.co.uk/health/kids
A general site with lots of body information.

http://bart.northnet.com.au/~amcgann/body
A look inside the human body – body guide and fact sheet.

www.bbc.co.uk/education/medicine/
A website that covers Galen, Vesalius, Harvey, Fleming, and others.

www.webgod.net/leonardo/Anatomy/Default.htm
Provides good selection of Leonardo's anatomical drawings.

www.virtualvermont.com/history/gage.html
Provides a full account of Phineas Gage and his accident.

www.metaphor.dk/guillotine/Pages/30sec.html
Dr. Beaurieux's account of Languille's beheading.

www.james.com/beaumont/dr_life.htm
About William Beaumont including his work with Alexis St. Martin.

www.yahooligans.com/content/ka/almanac/bodyfood/index.html
Body and food – an owner's almanac.

TRADITIONAL MEDICINE

Acupuncture Treating disorders by sticking needles into the skin at particular points to alter the flow of energy or Ch'i through invisible energy channels or meridians.

Aromatherapy Aiding relaxation, or treating disorders, with scented plant oils that are massaged into the body or added to bath water.

Ayurvedic medicine Traditional Indian system of medicine that aims to treat the whole person and prevent illness from occurring.

Chiropractic Relief of pain mainly by manipulating the joints of the backbone.

Herbal medicine Ancient practice of using healing properties of certain plants to treat illnesses. Still plays important part in both traditional Chinese and Indian medicine.

Homeopathy Treating disorders by giving patient a very dilute dose of a remedy that in a full strength dose would produce symptoms similar to the illness that is being treated.

Hydrotherapy Use of water – including whirlpool baths, showers, steam baths – to treat a disorder.

Naturopathy Treatment of the whole person by changing their diet or lifestyle, or by using other alternative therapies, in order to restore the body's "normal balance" and boost its ability to cure itself.

Osteopathy Diagnosis and treatment of disorders of the body's framework – bones, joints, ligaments, tendons, muscles, nerves – by, for example, manipulation, stretching, massage, and exercise.

Reflexology Massaging specific regions of the feet in order to treat disorders of parts of the body that are supposed to be related to those regions.

BODY GLOSSARY

Adolescence
Period during teenage years when children become adults.

Alveoli
Microscopic air bags inside the lungs through which oxygen enters the bloodstream.

Amputation
Surgical operation to remove a part of the body, such as an arm or leg.

Anesthetic
Drug used by doctors to stop the patient feeling pain during surgery.

Antibody
Substance released by the immune system to combat pathogens.

Antiseptic
Chemical rubbed on the skin to kill germs and prevent infection.

Blood vessel
Tube that carries blood through the body. The main types are arteries, veins, and capillaries.

Carbon dioxide
Gas, produced as a waste product of energy release, breathed out in air.

Cartilage
Tough, flexible material that forms parts of structures, such as the nose and larynx (voice box), and covers the ends of bones.

Cells
Tiny living units that are the basic building blocks of the body.

Cerebrum
The largest part of the brain which enables people to think and feel, and controls body movements.

Chromosome
One of 46 threadlike packages of DNA inside every body cell.

Disease
Breakdown in normal working of the body caused by pathogens or a problem inside the body.

DNA
The chemical found inside chromosomes, containing instructions to build and operate a cell.

Endocrine gland
A gland, such as the pituitary gland, that releases hormones into the bloodstream.

Enzyme
Chemical that greatly speeds up reactions, such as the breakdown of food during digestion.

Feces
Solid waste that remains after digestion, and is expelled from the body through the anus.

Fertilization
Joining together of the egg and sperm during reproduction.

Gene
Instruction needed to build and run a cell stored in the DNA in chromosomes.

Haemoglobin
Substance that carries oxygen in red blood cells.

Hormone
Chemical messenger produced by an endocrine gland, carried by blood.

Joint
Part of the skeleton where two or more bones meet.

Ligaments
Tough straps that hold bones together at joints.

Melanin
Brown pigment that colors skin

and hair.

Mitochondria
Structures inside cells that release energy from food.

MRI scan
Uses magnetism and radio waves to produce images of the body's insides.

Mucus
Thick, slippery fluid that lines the respiratory and digestive systems.

Muscle
Tissue that can contract and cause movement.

Nerve
Cablelike bundle of neurons that links all body parts to the brain and spinal cord.

Neurons
Nerve cells that make up the brain, spinal cord, and nerves, and carry electrical signals at high speed.

Nutrients
Substances in food that are useful to the body, including carbohydrates, fats, proteins, vitamins, and minerals.

Organ
Major body part, such as the heart or brain, made up of different tissues, with a specific role or roles.

Oxygen
Gas taken from breathed-in air and used by cells to release energy from food.

Pathogens
Disease-causing microscopic organisms such as bacteria or viruses.

Peristalsis
Waves of muscle contraction that push food through the digestive system.

Plasma
Liquid, colorless part of blood.

Puberty
Period during adolescence when the body grows and develops rapidly, and the reproductive system starts working.

Reflex
Automatic action such as swallowing, blinking, or pulling a hand away from a sharp object.

Spinal cord
Column of nervous tissue that relays nerve messages between the brain and body.

Stethoscope
Instrument used to listen to sounds made by body parts, such as the lungs and heart.

Sweat
Salty, waste liquid released onto the skin that helps to cool the body.

System
Group of linked organs that work together to do a particular job.

Tendon
Tough cord or sheet that links muscle to bone.

Tissue
Collection of similar cells that have one particular role.

Transplant
Operation to take an organ or tissues from one person and put them into another.

Ultrasound scan
Image produced by beaming sound waves into the body.

Urine
Waste liquid produced by the kidneys.

Villi
Tiny fingerlike projections from the small intestine wall that transfer digested food into the bloodstream.

X-rays
Invisible rays used to produce images of hard parts of the body, like bone.

INDEX

CREDITS

Dorling Kindersley would like to thank:
Dawn Davies-Cook and Joanna Pocock for design assistance; Almudena Diaz and Nomazwe Modonko for DTP assistance; and Kate Bradshaw for editorial help. Thanks also to Chris Bernstein for the index.

Additional photography by:
Geoff Brightling, Andy Crawford, Philip Dowell, John Garrett, Steve Gorton, Dave King, Time Ridley, Clive Streeter, Adrian Whicher, Jerry Young.

Richard Walker would like to thank:
Lucy Hurst, Ann Cannings, Fran Jones, Marcus James, and the rest of the team at DK responsible for this book, for their hard work, enthusiasm, creativity, and attention to detail.

Picture Credits